KILLERS
ONLINE

100 True Stories

by
Lori Carangelo

Access Press

ISBN: 9780942605532

contents

13
CRAIGSLIST CARNAGE - 115
(Craigslist.com)

*"Try to avoid getting involved with somebody
who's gonna need killing before it's over.
It may seem to you that it narrows the field somewhat, but be diligent."*
-Jill Conner Browne,
"The Sweet Potato Queens' Book of Love"

INTRODUCTION

Considering there are millions of Users on social media and classified ad sites, chances of being approached by someone with ulterior motives is no small risk, despite whatever precautions that you might take.

- 3% of online daters are psychopaths;
- 10% of members on free dating websites are scammers;
- 10% of sex offenders use online dating sites;
- 25% of rapists used online dating sites to seek out their next victim;
- nearly half of all murdered women are killed by romantic partners;
- 51% of online daters are already in a relationship;
- over 400 murders were linked to dating sites;
- **in 2016, over 101 murders were linked to Craigslist ads**

CRAIGSLIST:

In this book about 100 online killers (and a few rapists who met their attackers online), the largest number of online ad-related **MURDERS** are attributed to **Craigslist,** and so Craigslist murders fill the largest chapter in this book. From 1995 until 2018, Craigslist not only advertised garage sales that often resulted in prospective Buyers and Sellers being robbed, assaulted and even murdered, but also Craigslist ran Personals ads soliciting and offering sex of all types.

Advanced Interactive Media Group launched a **"Safe Trade Stations"** initiative to allow Buyer and Seller to meet at the police station. The initiative resulted in Craigslist closing its Personal ads sections when US Senate Bill H.R. 1865, "the sex trafficking bill" was enacted on April 11, 2018, enabling fines and prison terms of up to 10 years for websites which "unlawfully promote and facilitate" sex work, in addition to "unlawful sex acts with sex trafficking victims." Sex workers argue that online advertising of their services is safer for them as it keeps them off the streets as "independent" sex workers, instead of at the mercy of pimps for less money.

But under-18-year-olds can easily create or respond to social media ads, thereby becoming naïve targets.

FACEBOOK:

Out of a world population of 7.4-billion, at least 2.7-billion people use **Facebook**, **WhatsApp**, **Instagram** or **Messenger** *each month*. **Facebook** has been called a "virtual graveyard"of 30-to-50-million accounts that belong to *dead people* whose accounts live on in limbo due to no one with their password canceling them. Facebook is also a graveyard of victims who met their **KILLERS** on Facebook.

Anthropologist Robin Dunbar famously suggested people could maintain *"150 meaningful relationships"* at any one time and it's clear to Facebook that your "Friends" list is what makes Facebook valuable. In *"Facebook Needs a 'Reset' Button For Your Friend List"* (12-27-18), Kurt Wagner wrote: "I'm not trying to brag, but I have 981 Facebook friends. I could have a dinner with a different Facebook friend every night for nearly 3 years before I'd need to meet someone new... [but] I've also stopped sharing personal things about *myself* because I don't necessarily want all 981 people to see them." [Move over, Kurt, this writer currently has over 3,500 Facebook Friends as a potential market for self-promotion of my books, with over 400 "followers" and counting]. Wagner explained: "This isn't an accident. Facebook has spent the past 14 years encouraging users to have as many friends as possible… More friends means more things for you to see on Facebook and more time spent using the service, which has turned **Facebook** into an advertising empire. It's why all kinds of other companies, from **Spotify** to **Yelp** to **Tinder**, let people log in to their apps using a Facebook profile. Building a network of connections is hard for small businesses, so a lot of internet companies encourage customers to port one over from Facebook. In theory, if you reduce your Friends you'll start to see more from the people you're closest to. You can 'Un-friend' people, though you have to do this one friend at a time, but you'll feel horribly guilty when you're done." [Or you might push a rejection-sensitive "friend" over the edge to **MURDER you** – as documented by news stories in the Facebook chapter of this book.

POPULAR DATING APPS:

In the U.S., online dating is $3-billion dollar a year market. **Plenty of Fish (POF)** is an online dating service that has at least **100-million** users, with an estimated 500,000 paid members. And is free to register and contact other members. About 3.5-million are daily active users, about 85% of whom use the service via the mobile app. Popular in Canada, United Kingdom, Ireland, Australia, New Zealand, Brazil, and the United States, and is available in 9 languages. POF, founded by Markus Frind, is owned by **PlentyOfFish** Media Inc.

Other dating/hookup websites, **Match.com, Tinder, OKCupid, Hinge, Pairs, Meetic,** and **Two**, are all properties of The Match Group founded in 1995 by Gary Kremen with Users in 25 countries:

> 32% of Match Group users are Millennials;
> 39% are Gen X;
> 27% are Boomers;
> 38% are Single Parents;
> 1-million babies have resulted from Match.com connections.

Before logging on to any dating or hookup site, consider the following:

(1) People lie in their online profiles - including on the Christian-oriented date site, **eHarmony** (founded by Neil Clark Warren in Y-2000), the largest date site geared toward marriage and long term relationships, where dating 6 partners at once is now normal, and where rapists and a network of scammers from Nigeria to Turkey target women via that site. Both eHarmony and J-Date for Jewish singles are owned by Sparks Network (JDate was founded by David Yarus in 2014). In a study conducted by the global research agency, Opinion Matters, of over 1,000 online dates in the U.S. and U.K., they found:

- **53% of U.S.** participants admitted they lied in their dating profile
- **20% of women** posted photos of their younger selves; men also, but to lesser extent;
- **40% of men** lied about their financial situation, job, etc. as did 1/3 of women; while one's net worth is no predictor of a person's values, a "white lie" may be hiding a bigger lie.

Lies by Paul Guadalupe Gonzales, 45, the Los Angeles "**Dine-and-Dash Dater**" enabled him to lure women to nice restaurants, order food, and vanish – sticking his victims with the bill but numerous other scams have bilked unsuspecting women out of their money and tricked men into becoming unintended sugar daddies.

(2) Relationships that begin online don't last. According to a Michigan State University survey, relationships that began online were **28%** more likely to break down in the first year than those who first met face-to-face. Only 5% of couples who first met online were in committed relationships or marriages; couples are more judgmental and more inclined to eliminate not-quite perfect candidates than if they had met the same person face to face.

(3) Frequency: On average, men are more eager for sex than women - including solo sex (masturbation) and sex with an opposite-sex or same-sex partner.   Men assume that if a woman has an online dating presence she's interested in sleeping with relative strangers. So she is likely to receive rude messages from horny guys, sexual requests, "dick pics," and creepy vibes. While sexual **frequency** among married couples occurs "**1.25** times per week," in most studies single men had far more sexual partners than single women. Women had **one** sex partner per year, while men had **at least 6** sex partners. The **frequency** of sex for 18-29 year olds was **2.15** times per week; for 30-39 year olds it was **1.65** times per week; and for 40-49 year olds it was **1.33** times per week – which is not to say that seniors are not active, regardless of functionality. But, at least in the younger generation, men are 3 times more likely to achieve orgasm than women. **Sex Addiction** with either one or multiple partners is determined by the extent to which sex interferes with or becomes a priority and detriment in one's daily life.

What is "not normal" in 2020? Sex "hookup" apps proliferate because the demand means profit. A smorgasbord of what used to be publicly taboo is now publicly acceptable, or at least available, available online. The following are still considered *"not* normal" (with the percentage of people practicing it): **Voyeurism** (34.5%); **Festishism** (26.3%); **Exhibitionism** (sex with partner while someone else watches - 30.6%); **Frotteurism** (rubbing against a person, usually in public, without their permission – 26.1%); **Masochism** (19.2%); **Sadism** (5.5%); **Transvestism** (4.9%); **Sex with a child** (0.4%). **Bestiality** was not mentioned in that survey, but is part of the repertoire on porn video sites, and it's a good bet that the law isn't going to categorize our four-legged friends as "consenting." **Erotic Asphyxiation** – intentional, consensual restriction of oxygen to the brain by strangling one's partner, or one's self, for sexual arousal – has been blamed for accidental deaths... and intentional murders.

However, those who do seek a wider variety of sexual encounters, a list of **"300 Apps for Dating and Sexual Encounters"** is included at the end of this book and one has only to Google to find such local versions.

What is "normal" in 2020? It used to be confined to the prostitute's playbook, Jon Voight received it on screen in "Midnight Cowboy" (1969), then Jane Fonda gave it in "Coming Home" (1978), but **oral sex** is still more

12

"a matter of personal taste." While most, but not all, **homosexual** men have engaged in **anal sex** at some point, surveys say the overwhelmingly majority engaged in both "insertive and receptive" intercourse. One survey found that, for **heterosexual** couples, 10% of women engaged in **anal sex**. State **Sodomy** laws were intended to deem sex acts such as anal copulation, oral

sex, bestiality, as "unnatural" or "immoral" in order to also criminalizing homosexuals, but such laws are rarely spelled out and are now typically applied only in non-consensual cases of Rape or Sexual Assault.

Statutory Rape statutes intended to protect under-age girls from being victimized by older men, can also result jail time for a 15-year old's 17-year old boyfriend when her pissed off parents find out they've been having sex.

Men, more than women, were willing to test fantasies of threesomes, foursomes or "group sex," but "No" is still "No" when determining who or how many are "consenting." Proving it is another matter that even the #MeToo movement is wrestling with as powerful men are being publicly accused of sexual assault and Rape without due process. And as headlines now reveal, sex trafficking of women and children is a pastime of not only your common street pimp but also of people in high places. Internet has just made it more pervasive to meet the demand of a large market.

In **"How To Not Get Killed By Your Tinder Date,"** Jaya Powell suggests meeting in a public place and staying sober so as not to be vulnerable, and to first make sure s/he is who s/he says s/he is. Refuse to meet anyone who will not share their full name and where they are from. A Google search of a name may bring up a photo with his/her wife/husband, or a court record or newsclip of a past arrest, but a background check is often cheap enough, from online companies, although even the most reputable service does not guarantee that they are providing the most current information. [**MyLife.com** is notorious for publicly listing not only outdated addresses and backgrounds, but also **false** information harvested from internet sites that may not even be about the person named. So search your own name on MyLife.com and if you didn't provide your information and/or it's false, demand removal in case YOUR date checks YOUR background.]

Also, inform a friend - someone ready and waiting to pick up and rescue you - as to who you're meeting and if you then go elsewhere. Agree on code phrases such as *"Everything is fine"* in case things go wrong, so when the friend can call you back, without tipping off your date, you have an excuse to bail.

For those who cannot have sex, or aren't interested in sex, but want a close or committed relationship, there's **Asexualistic.com**. Unfortunately, it's a rare app and most members are surprisingly young, rather than seniors with

erectile dysfunction (ED), and, not surprisingly, most are female.

OKCupid.com, one of the more popular free date sites, does provide the option of selecting "Asexual" when constructing one's profile.

GRINDR:

Grindr, (founded by Joel Simkhair, who was born in Tel Aviv and who is openly gay), now in its 10th year, has been hailed as "a cure for gay loneliness and a symbol of sexual liberation." Part of Grindr's allure is that it doesn't force you to *identify* yourself and, in a large city, you can have solely **transactional sex** with a stranger "within 20 minutes." But Grindr and other hook-up apps carry more risk of violence and disease that can occur within the context of any casual sex encounter via dating/sex apps, sex parties, bars and clubs, and can be connected to "overlapping" forms of violence, including "hate" violence, intimate partner violence, sexual violence, or simple revenge. Between 2016 and 2017, more than 1,000 men on Grindr approached Matthew Herrick, indicating they expected to buy drugs and/or have violent sex with him, as his Grndr profile suggested. But Herrick never created a profile. It was actually his "ex" *impersonating* Herrick in an attempt to harass him. Worse, Grindr ignored Herrick's requests to remove it. The harassing "ex" was ultimately arrested in 2017.

Of greater concern, Grindr has been the perfect conduit for luring gays to orchestrate **Theft, Rape, Torture, and MURDER** and apparent *deliberate transmission of HIV to unknowing partners*.

While Grindr is the largest site of its kind, there are many other gay-oriented apps that carry the same risk of someone specifically targeting gays. And one site, **Backpage.com**, crossed the line into human trafficking and was shut down by the FBI (FYI, Backpage stories are also included in this book).

Screen names and anonymity allege to protect privacy – yours and theirs – but they also shield hoaxters, sexual predators, and **KILLERS,** as the following news stories evidence (see Bibliography for sources).

Be afraid, be very afraid, be smart , and be safe.

1.
FACEBOOK
FATALITIES
(Facebook.com)

Peter Chapman and Ashleigh Hall

FATAL FRIENDING

Ashleigh Hall, 17, had just begun her first year at Darlington College in the United Kingdom. She was taking a child care course and planning a career as child minder or nursery nurse. The chubby but pretty teenager had a pleasant disposition so was well-liked by her friends. Her mother, Andrea Hall, 39, called Ashleigh the most sensible, level-headed of her four daughters, although, like other teenagers, she was struggling with self esteem. Like other teenagers, a cell phone and the Internet and Facebook "friending" were major features of Ashleigh's daily life. She had 400 Facebook Friends, including friends-of-friends, all of whom she "more or less" knew. And then one day the Facebook photo of a handsome, shirtless, new boy caught her attention. His screen name was "D.J. Pete" and his profile said he was 17. It was mid-October when they began exchanging private messages. He told her his real name was **Pete Cartwright** and that he had had a privileged but lonely upbringing.

D.J. Pete, or **Pete Cartwright,** was, in fact, **Peter Chapman**, and he was actually 33, an emaciated, almost toothless, homeless man living in his car. His fake Facebook profile had attracted interest from 14,600 visitors, almost 3,000 becoming online "friends," all of whom were females ranging from the age of 13 to 31.   He would attempt to redirect them to private chat rooms where he would invite them to provide sexually explicit details. Chapman set up two profiles on the Netlog site and had others on at least 9 other sites.

Chapman had been raised by his grandparents – a kinship adoption. He grew up in the U.K., in Stockton-on-Tees, where former shipbuilding, heavy engineering, chemicals and steel industries had declined, leaving poverty in its wake. As with most adoptees, not much was shared with Peter about his parents and that bothered him throughout his childhood. He couldn't help but wonder, was his "Mum" a prostitute who so easily rejected and abandoned him?   In 1992, at 15, he was the subject of a sexual assault investigation. Four years later, Chapman was accused of raping a girl he had befriended. She became pregnant but the allegations were later dropped. At 19, In December 1996, he found himself before Teesside Crown Court accused of attacking two teenage prostitutes. He had stolen a car, fitted it with false number plates, and cruised the streets of Middlesbrough before picking up a 17-year-old street girl, driving her to County Durham and raping her at knife point. Two days later he did exactly the same thing to another prostitute. Chapman was sentenced to 7 years' imprisonment. In 2002 he was arrested by Cheshire Police for Rape and Kidnap of a prostitute in Ellesmere Port. The case was discontinued.

On October 25, 2009, Ashleigh Hall was in an obviously good mood because "DJ Pete" wanted to meet her. In order to entice her into his car, he texted her that "his dad" would pick her up, which somehow made her feel safe. The two agreed to keep the rendezvous secret for now, lest her mother disapprove of a blind date. So Ashleigh told her mother she was going to spend that Sunday night at a friend's house. The last message from D.J. Pete said *"He's on his way now, Babe."* It was already dark at 7:30 PM when Ashleigh threw some clothes into her bag as the car pulled up. *"He's here now,"* she texted back, and hurried off into the night, her heart pounding in anticipation. The older looking driver reached across the passenger seat and opened the door for her. She had been inside his vehicle no longer than a heartbeat when he attacked her. Ashleigh's body was found dumped in a farmer's field near Sedgefield, County Durham. She had been brutally raped, her arms were bound and tape was put over her face, suffocating her to death.

Chapman confessed to the murder of Ashleigh Hall to a custody officer:
"I killed someone last night. I need to tell somebody where the body is. It hasn't been reported yet."   Chapman was jailed for 45 years for the Kidnap, Rape and Murder of 17-year old Ashleigh Hall.

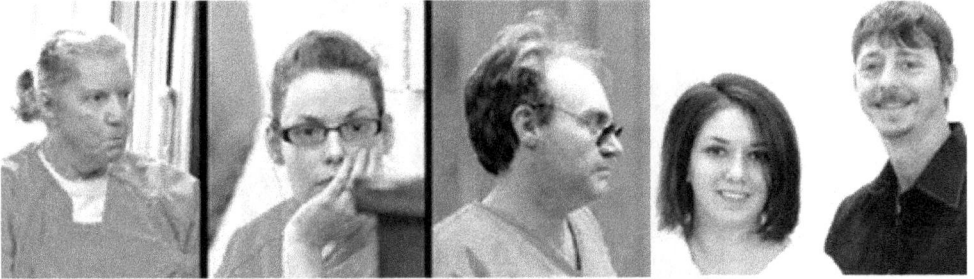

Barbara Potter, Jenelle Potter, Jamie Curd   Jean Hayworth, Bill Payne

UGLY UN-FRIENDINGS

Barbara Potter, 64, and her daughter, **Jenelle Potter**, 35, both of Mountain City, Tennessee, were charged with the shooting deaths of **Billy Clay Payne**, 36, and **Billie Jean Hayworth**, 23, in 2012, The victims were found inside their home with their 7-month-old son who covered in blood but alive.

The Johnson City Press reports that two other defendants, **Marvin Enoch "Buddy" Potter, 60,** and **Jamie Lynn Curd**, 38, were also charged two counts of First Degree Murder. Marvin Potter, Jenelle Potter's father, is already serving two life sentences for the slayings. Curd reached a plea agreement. Assistant District Attorney General Dennis Brooks said the killings happened after Jenelle Potter was "un-friended" by the Hayworth-Payne couple on <u>Facebook</u>.

During opening statements, Brooks set the stage for the killings, which he said were based on threats Jenelle Potter had created. Brooks described her as a bored, lonely 30-something who created several online personas. Hundreds of emails from the Potter's family computer "spewing hate" toward Hayworth were discovered. Prosecutors presented testimony from six witnesses in the case, including Tennessee Bureau of Investigation Agent Scott Lott. Lott told the jury the big break in the case came about a week after the killings when Curd admitted to investigators he participated in the murders, implicating Marvin Potter. Both Potter women faced Life in prison.

It wasn't the first time someone fell victim to a <u>Facebook</u> "un-friending"...

A K2FRAZIER DRAMA FILM WRITTEN & DIRECTED BY KERRY-ANN FRAZIER

FRIEND REQUEST

DO YOU KNOW WHO'S ON THE OTHER SIDE?

WILL MOLEON · ANTOINETTE BAILEY · RAYLENE GILL· ANDREW LAUCK

JAINA WRITX   SKYE CAMERON MYERS   EMMA ROSE GILL   JORDAN BUIE

STRANGER THAN FICTION

There have been fiction movies capitalizing on true incidents of Facebook-related murders, but the true stories are even stranger than fiction.

Lashawndra Harris (photo not available), from Quincy, Louisiana, was charged with 5 murders after killing 5 people when they did not accept her friend request on Facebook. Harris had been dubbed by police as **"The Facebook Friend Request Killer'** because at the scene of every murder a card was left on the victim's body that showed the <u>Facebook</u> logo along with the button with which you can accept or deny a friend request.

Detective Paul Horner of the DeQuincy Police Department explained how Harris was finally apprehended. *"She is probably the worst serial killer in the history of serial killers. At every murder scene she would leave a 'calling card' on the bodies with scribbled words written on each one such as, 'Maybe next time you'll be my friend on <u>Facebook</u> motherf*cker', or 'Who's got more friends on Facebook now b*tch!',"* Horner said. "All of the people who were murdered lived in the same apartment building or were people that knew Harris personally. **Leron Jenkins** who was a neighbor of Harris said he was approached by her just days before the arrest. *"I didn't like her, she was scary. She told me that if I didn't accept her friend request on <u>Facebook</u> she would literally cut my balls off. So, long story short, I accepted her friend request."*

Rebecca Aylward and Joshua Davies

DEADLY DARE

Joshua Davies, 16, was an academically gifted boy from a church-going family. Joshua met **Rebecca Aylward** when he was 11 and they began going out together in 2009 until Rebecca ended the relationship after 3 months. In October 2010, Joshua asked Rebecca, then 15, to see each other again. In the weeks leading up to Rebecca's murder, Joshua had posted messages on Facebook saying he wanted to kill Rebecca. His 900 Facebook Friends thought he was joking; he then asked *"What would you do if I actually killed her?"* The friend replied *"Oh, I would buy you breakfast."*

At their first meeting, Joshua lured Rebecca to a secluded spot, tried unsuccessfully to break her neck, then, to quiet her screams, smashed in her skull with a large rock.

After the murder, Joshua posted a Facebook update:
"I enjoyed a rather good day and a lovely breakfast."

Kayleigh Haywood

Luke Harlow, Stephen Beadman

WELL GROOMED FOR DEATH

The murder of **Kayleigh Haywood**, 15, from Measham, Leicestershire, took place following 2600 mostly text messages in two weeks of online grooming by **Luke Harlow**, 27, who had contacted her via Facebook. Believing Harlow was then her boyfriend, Haywood was lured to Harlow's flat and agreed to stay with him there on Friday the 13th in November 2015.

As Haywood fled from Harlow's flat, naked from the waist down, Harlow's next door neighbor, **Stephen Beadman**, 29, who had been watching extreme porn videos, chased her. Although she fought him, he overpowered her, taking her across the road where he raped her before making her walk a mile-and-a-half on rough ground to where he battered her to death with a brick. Her body was found 3 days later with so many facial injuries that she had to be identified through her dental records.

Beadman was convicted of Murder and sentenced to Life in Prison, although he could be released in 35 years. Harlow was convicted of sexually touching and falsely imprisoning Haywood and grooming her and 2 other 15 year old girls. One of those girls told police she still loves Harlow. Leicestershire Police produced a 15-minute video, *"Kayleigh's Love Story"* which was shown to school children to warn the about online grooming and a second documentary, titled *"Murder on the Internet"* was screened on Channel 5 TV.

Eddie Leal; Manuel Edmundo Guzman Jr.; alleged Rebecca Santhiago

APRIL FOOL

In May 2011, **Eddie Leal,** 23, was captivated by the seductive **Rebecca Santhiago,** 23, on <u>Facebook</u>.

Eddie Leal was born in the small desert town of Hemet, California, in 1987 but his life was spent in the San Jacinto valley. While still a very young child, Eddie developed a love for boxing as result of being trained to box by his father, Gilbert Ralph Leal. Although small in stature, Eddie was a determined and tenacious and competed in numerous boxing fights. An extremely generous, courteous, soft spoken, polite and very affectionate young man, Eddie loved to give back to the community. He and his father volunteered thousands of hours with Cops for Kids, a program designed to keep kids off the streets. They trained numerous kids, as well as cops, and they too became boxers. The boxing students became part of a boxing community dubbed "Team Leal" that won many competitions. In addition to his community work and his work as a student tutor, Eddie also worked at the Power House Gym as a personal trainer. Eddie's life was one of giving. He gave not only to his community, but also his mother, father, and brother Gilbert. He did not know how to use the word "no." During high school, he was good at math and, at 23, Eddie wanted to become a teacher but he had just begun fighting professionally as a bantamweight. He was a member of the Advanced Via Individual Determination Club (AVID), and then tutored middle and high school students who had aspirations of going on to college. According to his mother, Celia Leal, "Eddie was a good boy and a good son." He worked at an Arco AM-PM store in Hemet and in San Jacinto for about a year. Friends and co-workers described him as "a very nice, very kind, very gracious person – always in a good mood."

According to Rebecca Santhiago's Facebook profile, she was a student at Mt. San Jacinto College in Riverside and had 137 Facebook friends. Rebecca's Facebook page displayed a photo of the attractive, sweet faced, curvaceous, seductively smiling woman with long dark hair in a skin-tight white mini-dress sufficiently low-cut to show off her ample cleavage. There was also a photo which prominently focused on her butt which was covered only by a skimpy thong. She described herself as a single 23-year-old whose birthday was April 1, 1989 – April Fool's Day – and that she "loves to kick it at house parties or clubs" and wants to meet men who will "show some love." Eddie eagerly agreed to meet Rebecca near a park in San Jacinto in the early morning hours on May 20, 2011. Eddie's computer saved the MapQuest directions to their rendevous location which he had written on the back of an envelope that he took with him. His computer also revealed his communications with Rebecca Santhiago who asked Leal to bring her a "Four Loko," a caffeinated alcoholic beverage. She told Leal to pick up her brother, who would direct him to a liquor store. Leal typed at 1:50 a.m. that he would be at the park in about 10 minutes.

Around 2 a.m., Eddie drove his Toyota Corolla to the 1900 block of Roanoke Street, near Ivy Crest Drive. A resident heard gunfire and called 911. Deputies arrived to find Leal slumped over in his driver's seat, his car still in drive after striking a parked vehicle. Eddie Leal was dead, shot in the back. He apparently had tried to call 911 from his cell phone at 2:10. All of the bullets that hit him came from the same semi-automatic gun. A search of Eddie's computer by Sheriff's detectives revealed he had been in contact with a woman named Rebecca Santhiago. At the time of the Leal-Santhiago contacts, **Manuel Edmundo Guzman, Jr.**, 17, known as "Tito," was living at home with his mother and two sisters when he created a Facebook account. When Guzman's computer was confiscated, it revealed communications, allegedly by Rebecca Santhiago with Eddie Leal. Santhiago was not what she appeared to be. Guzman had posed as Rebecca Santhiago and used the profile to engage three other young men in chat. When the other men asked who she would be with, or if she had a phone number, the conversation ended. The only motive offered was that Guzman murdered Eddie Leal for a "thrill kill." Guzman was convicted of Murder in the First Degree with a special circumstance of lying in wait. Because he was 17 at the time of the murder, and therefore not eligible for the Death Penalty, he was sentenced to Life in prison without the possibility of parole.

"Nothing is so common as the wish to be remarkable."
-William Shakespeare

Nicole Cable and Kyle Dube

FINAL HOOKUP

Nichole Cable was 15 when she was last seen alive. **Kyle Dube**, 20, had posted a picture of her on his Facebook page with the following message: *"Please help this family get back together. Nichole wherever you are, I hope you're safe."* The next day, he posted another picture and the words: *"Help find Nichole Cable."*

Kyle Dube was born in Presque Isle, Maine, was a student in automotive technology at Eastern Maine Community College in Bangor in 2011-12. and listed his employer as the Getchell Agency, a company in Bangor that provides a range of services to people with disabilities. He also worked at a full-service gas station in Bangor, called Doc's. On June 2012, Dube led police on a high-speed chase on I-95 north of Bangor. His motorcycle was clocked at more than 130 mph before he slowed down and hit a police cruiser. He was charged with Driving To Endanger, Eluding An Officer and Criminal Speeding. Dube had tried to elude the police because he was scared his parents would find out he had gotten a ticket.

Nichole Cable lived in Glenburn, which borders Orono, and went to Old Town High School. A friend of Cable said she and Dube had been hanging out together for several weeks. Dube's Facebook page named another woman as his girlfriend and shows pictures of the two together. A post by

Dube, posted on May 13, the day after Cable disappeared: *"OK so I don't like [drama]. Let's get things straight. I KYLE DUBE is and always will be with (the named girlfriend). We have had are ups and downs but we have worked them out so stop talking to me if [you're] trying to flirt - and guys you better stop hitting on (my girlfriend). I'm fucking crazy when I get pissed off and I'm about there."* One week after that Facebook posting about Nichole Cable, police announced that they had discovered the girl's body in a wooded area in Old Town.

Dube had turned himself in to police on unrelated charges from April 2011 for Theft and Burglary of a Motor Vehicle, and for Theft in December 2012. He pleaded guilty in both cases and paid fines, intending to begin serving a 90-day jail sentence related to those charges, but his timing was unfortunate. Police said they had enough evidence to also charge him with Cable's murder. Police said that, shortly before she disappeared, Cable planned to connect with a man she had met on Facebook, named **Bryan Butterfield**. Investigators learned that Dube had posed as "Bryan Butterfield" on Facebook and offered Cable marijuana before she disappeared on May 12, 2013. Cable went to meet Butterfield, who was actually Dube, and he was waiting for her with a mask over his face. Dube had planned to stage an abduction and then "rescue" Cable *to make himself appear to be a "hero."* In text messages, Cable told her current boyfriend that she had first met a man named Dube on May 11, but that he had groped her. She said she tried pushing Dube off her but he wouldn't stop and ended up leaving a bite mark. Cable nevertheless remained friendly with Dube, continuing to text him on May 12. Not knowing Dube had created "Butterfield," she told Dube that she was going to meet a man named Butterfield to get a "free 20 bag" but expressed reservations about meeting Butterfield at the end of her dirt road, asking Dube *"Is it alright to be a little scared?"* Dube texted back, *"No I wouldn't be."* Police traced the fake Facebook profile for Butterfield to Dube's home and found evidence of a struggle and a chase. Cable had lost her sneakers as she apparently tried to flee. A mask bearing Dube's DNA was discovered on the ground and Dube had scratches on his face.

Dube was charged with Kidnapping and Murder. His lawyer, Stephen Smith, tried to keep the documents under seal, but the judge allowed some of them to be released after some redactions. According to state police, Dube told others that he had intended to abduct Cable using a mask and duct tape and then return to find her, becoming *a hero, but,* instead, he found her dead after binding her with duct tape and putting her body in the bed of his father's pickup. Cable's mother, Kristin Wiley, said that she intends to work with law enforcement to raise awareness of the potential perils of social media and how to stay safe online.

Nichole Okrzesik, James Ayers, Juliana Mensch

IT'S COMPLICATED

James Ayers, 32, and **Nichole Okrzesik**, 23 were having a heated <u>Facebook</u> exchange. *"You held her down... you're guilty of murder too,"* read the Facebook message. In their many messages on <u>Facebook</u> it appeared Ayres was threatening to confess to police about a murder:
Ayers: *"I only did what I did to Julie for you but you still continue to be unfaithful.*
Okrzesik: *"I'm   being   honest   im   scared   of   you"*
Ayers: *"Are you coming home, if not I'll just turn us both in"*
Okrzesik: *"im scared of you right now, ya I told you if you calm down I will"*
At no point in the hundreds of messages did Okrzesik deny any involvement in the murder. March 27, 2012, Ayers wrote: *"We have to figure this out, I'm not going to but if the smell gets worse we're fucked."*
Okrzesik: *"Cant we just go dump it somewhere then take off?"*

Then James Ayers told a friend he strangled **Juliana Mensch,** 18, after Nichole Okrzesik *"tried to break her neck, couldn't do it, and she [Juliana] started screaming."* And Okrzesik's did a Google search for "What's on those rags that make people pass out"; "ways to kill people in their sleep"; "could you kill someone in their sleep and no one would think it was murder"; "how to suffocate someone"

Ayers was charged with First Degree Murder on March 29, 2012, and Okrzesik was also arrested for Murder six weeks later on May 10.

Natasha Plummer and son, Octavia Barnett – Lineten Belizaire

HI HONEY, I'M HOME

Octavia Barnett, 21, had threatened her ex-boyfriend, **Lineten Belizaire,** 21, that she would take him to court and force him to start paying to support his baby. Belizaire allegedly had several "baby mamas," as one witness put it, and complained that he would "hurt or kill" the next woman who tried to nail him for child support.

On January 21, 2012, Barnett wrote in a <u>Facebook </u>post to her son, *"Your daddy came back from out of town from 4 months [sic] ago... better late than never."* Barnett also stated that **Belizaire** was at the door of her Florida home. A few minutes later, Barnett was shot dead, along with her friend **Natasha Plummer** and **Plummer's 6-month old son, Carlton Stringer Jr.** The only survivor in the murder was Barnett's 11-month old son, Ladinian, whose father is believed Belizaire. The other child died in his mother's arms. A neighbor living below said that she heard gunshots and saw blood dripping through the ceiling.

Belizaire was first arrested in 2012, but released when a grand jury failed to indict him because he had not been read his Miranda rights; he was later re-arrested, based on "new evidence," but pleaded "not guilty" to 3 counts of Second Degree Murder With a Firearm in the triple homicide of Octavia Barnett, Natasha Plummer and her baby Carlton Stringer Jr. and was released on $75,000 bond that his family helped him raise. He was also sentenced to 11 Years in federal prison for Tax Fraud in an unrelated case and this time was jailed without bond. No record of any further action regarding the triple murder charges can be found.

Steve Stephens, Robert Godwin Sr.;   <u>Facebook</u> Video of Stevens Killing Godwin

CAUGHT ON CAMERA

Steve Stephens, 37, a vocational specialist at Beech Book, a behavioral health agency, randomly shot to death **Robert Godwin, Sr.**, 74, on Easter Sunday, April 16, 2017, while Godwin was walking on a sidewalk in the Glenville neighborhood of Cleveland, Ohio. In the video which began while Stephens was in his car, stating he had "snapped," claiming responsibility for 13 murders, and warning there was going to be a 14th (although police were not aware of any other victims) and that he would keep killing until caught by police. He blamed a woman named Joy Lane, with whom he had a romantic relationship, for his state of mind. Seconds before the shooting, Stephens exited his car, approached Godwin who he asked to say the name "Joy Lane." Confused, Godwin asked "Joy Lane?" And Stephens said "She's the reason why this is about to happen to you" as he fatally shot Godwin. Stephens posted a cell phone video of the shooting on his <u>Facebook</u> account, which was copied to many media outlets. The Washington Post, New York Times and other media dubbed Stephens "*The Facebook Killer.*"

On April 18, Stephens pulled into the drive-through of a MacDonald's restaurant in Erie County, Pennsylvania, 100 miles from the location of the shooting, where a MacDonald's employee recognized Stephens from news reports and stalled him by stating that his fries were still cooking while police were called. Stephens, wary, left without his fries, but as Stephens pulled away from the restaurant, state police gave chase and performed a tactical maneuver that brought Stephens' car to a stop. As police approached his car, Stephens shot himself in the head and died instantly. The <u>Facebook</u> video was taken down.

Jennifer Harris

UNFRIENDLY FIRE

Jennifer Christine Harris, 30, of Des Moines, Iowa, was arrested on November 1, 2011 and charged with First Degree Arson for allegedly setting the October 27, 2011 fire to the Iowa home **of Nikki Rasmussen,** an old friend, while Nikki and her husband Bill were asleep inside the home. Luckily, the couple escaped unharmed, just as the fire began melting the siding on the house.

According to Nikki, Harris was angry **because Nikki ended their friendship by un-friending her on <u>Facebook</u>.**

Jasmine Nunez and Andres Ceballos

A FLAMING AFFAIR

Jasmine Maxine Nunez was a pretty, 22-year-old Hispanic woman. "Facebook was her life," her sister Melanie says. She had about 1,200 friends on the network. She was attending the Mandl School for medical assistants and had a part-time job as a dental receptionist, but wanted to be a surgical technician. One day, Jasmine was at the airport trying to catch a flight out of New York, but she missed the plane. **Andres Ceballos,** 26, was working security at the airport although he had studied at Cornell. Ever since they met, he was always surprising her with flowers." Like Jasmine, Andres was also an avid Facebook and Twitter user. Andres tried his luck at open mic as a standup comic at the Times Square Arts Center. On Feb. 11 2011, after the comedy club, they went to a nightclub where Andres became upset about a guy who danced with Jasmine and she was upset because he invited his ex-girlfriend among friends who came with them. Then Jasmine disappeared.

A badly burned body was found in James Baird State Park, in upstate New York, 7 days after Jasmine disappeared. Firefighters saw her lying in the grass, wearing Levi's 524 jeans, a cami shirt and Victoria's Secret underwear. She was, at first, unidentifiable. But there was a tattoo on her lower back. After leaving their Bronx apartment and dumping Jasmine's body in a park upstate and driving to Virginia Beach, Andres had also somehow bought a gun in Vermont. When the cops pulled him over for a routine traffic stop, he left the car, ran on foot into a field, and shot himself. He died at the scene.

"That's why crazy people are so dangerous.
You think they're nice until they're chaining you up in the garage."
-Michael Buckley,
in "The Fairy-Tale Detectives."

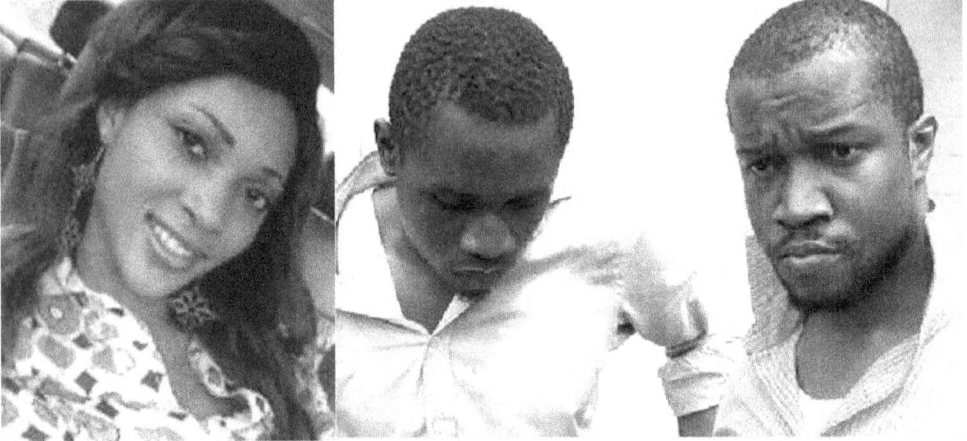

Cynthia Osokogu, Okumi Nwbufor Ejike Olisaeloka

NIGERIAN STALKER KILLER

Cynthia Udoku Osokogu, a 24-year old Nigerian fashion model and dress store owner, had, for months, chatted through her Blackberry and through Facebook with **Okwumi Echezona Nwabufor,** and soon she had also "friended" his cousin, **Ejike Ilechukwu Olisaeloka.** Police say Nwabufor told Cynthia that he was a student at Lagos State University in Nigeria but that he had connections and could help her with her fashion business. What Cynthia didn't know was that Nwabufor had actually been stalking her for months, patiently gaining her confidence through frequent chats and postings. Eventually, Nwabufor made Cynthia an offer that seemed too good to be true. He offered to buy her a plane ticket and to put her up in a nice hotel if she would come to Lagos to meet with his business associates. When Cynthia arrived in Lagos, she was taken to a hotel just outside of town. There, she was drugged, beaten, sexually assaulted and finally, murdered. She was targeted, police say, because the suspects had discovered that she was the daughter of a retired Nigerian Army general. They assumed that she would come to Lagos with cash, a large bank account and jewelry and felt that they could make some quick money out of her." But her brother, Kenneth Osokogu, says that Cynthia never carried any large sums of cash. "She doesn't even have an ATM card; she used a checkbook," he said.

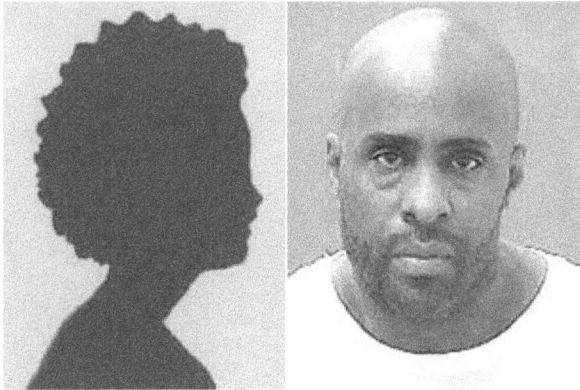

Lois Smyth (victim, photo not available) and Kenneth Brunetti

MARYLAND STALKER KILLER

Kenneth Todd Brunetti, 41, (photo) and **Lois Jean Vance Smyth**, then 40, who were childhood friends, reconnected on Facebook. He and Smyth developed a brief relationship while he was still on probation for a carjacking conviction. Even though Lois' sister, Janet Vance did not know Brunetti's record, she realized quickly that his relationship with her sister had taken a dark turn. Once, she heard him screaming and demanding to know who Lois was on the phone with. "She had been trying to end it," Vance said, "but he threatened her when she did" and he continued to **stalk** her. Janet advised Lois to report the incident to police. Instead, Janet promised she would stop seeing Brunetti. "She figured everything would be fine. She always thought everything would be OK."

On May 29, 2011, just days after Lois promised Janet to stop seeing him, Brunetti invited her to go to a cookout in Leakin Park. When they got there, he walked her down to a wooded area, fatally shot her in the head, stole her car and bank card, withdrew $700 from her account and went off to enjoy a crab dinner with friends just a few miles from the murder scene. A jogger discovered Smyth's body a few hours later.

When police arrested Brunetti it was on a violation-of-probation stemming from the car-jacking case, and they found Brunetti getting into Smyth's car. A Baltimore circuit judge sentenced Brunetti to Life plus 25 Years in Prison for Lois Smyth's murder, sentence to begin after he completes a 9-year sentence for violating his probation in the armed car-jacking case.

Nona Belomesoff, Christopher Dannevig

NSW STALKER KILLER

Christopher James Dannevig, 22, of New South Wales, pleaded guilty to Murder of Australian student, **Nona Belomesoff**, 18, after **stalking** her, just as Cynthia Osokogu had been stalked, through <u>Facebook</u>.

Just 8 days after his release on parole for kidnapping another young woman in 2009, Dannevig sent Nona a "friend" request. On learning that she was passionate about animal welfare, he created his Facebook account under the name of **Jason Green**. He told her he was a team leader at the NSW Wildlife Information Rescue Education Service (WIRES) and offered her a job.

In the guise of WIRES training, he then took her into the bushland on 5 occasions before killing her on May 12, 2010, by hitting her on her head with rocks and holding her under water for 2 minutes until she drowned.

Sarah Richardson and Edward Richardson

CYBER JEALOUSY MURDER

In late 2008, **Sarah Richardson,** 26, decided to change her Facebook "relationship status" from "married" to "single," Even though they were already separated, her husband, **Edward Richardson,** 41, did not like that.

He snuck into the Straffordshire, England home where she was staying with her parents, confronted Sarah with a knife while she slept and stabbed her to death. He then attempted to take his own life but was apprehended in time by authorities.

Edward Richardson received a 17-year prison sentence.

"Love is no inoculation against murder."
-N.K. Jemison, "The Obelisk Gate"

Hayley Jones and Brian Lewis

ADVANCE WARNING

On March 12, 2009, apparently **Hayley Jones,** 26, of South Wales, either hadn't hear or hadn't learned from the Richardson murder [see previous page] when she, too, changed her Facebook status to "single" and her overly possessive partner, **Brian Lewis**, 31, became suspicious of her spending too much time chatting on Facebook.

That's when Lewis told a friend at the local pub *"If I can't have her, then no f***** else will because I will kill her first."*

And he did – by strangling her to death in the home they shared with their 4 children.

*"From anonymous bullying to anonymous murder-for-hire,
the internet has something for every sick taste."*
-Kenneth Eade, "Killer.com"

Bullycide victim: Kameron Jacobson

MURDERS BY BULLYCIDE

Kameron Jacobsen, a 14-year-old freshman at Monroe-Woodbury High School in Central Valley, N.Y., died after taking his own life. Sources report that Kameron was tormented by Facebook bullies who taunted him because they thought he was gay.

Facebook issued this statement about the incidents, according to WNYW: "We are deeply saddened by the tragic deaths of these students, and our hearts go out to their family and friends. These cases serve as a painful reminder of how people can help others who are either bullied or show signs of distress on Facebook. We encourage them to notify us, and we work with third party support groups including the National Suicide Prevention Lifeline to reach out to people who may need help."

Bullycide victim: Audrie Pott

Audrie Pott, a 15-year-old, who was sexually assaulted by three 16-year old boys from Saratoga, California, took her own life after pictures of the attack were posted on <u>Facebook</u>. Pott hanged herself 8 days after the alleged assault, apparently despondent after photos of the attack were posted Facebook and shared among classmates at Saratoga High School. Pott's parents did not even know about the attack until after their daughter's death. "Other than murdering someone, the highest degree of a crime you could possibly do is to violate them in the worst of ways ... and then to effectively rub her face in it afterwards," Robert Allard, the attorney representing the girl's mother, father and step-mother, told the Associated Press. Allard said Pott was intoxicated and unconscious when the assault occurred, and that "there were multiple boys in the room with her."

This suicide occurred over Labor Day weekend in a prosperous Silicon Valley suburb on the west side of the Santa Clara Valley that is known for its wineries and high-end boutiques. The AP said Pott was at a sleepover at a friend's house when the unaccompanied teens got into liquor. At some point, Pott went upstairs to sleep and "woke up to the worst nightmare possible," Pott soon "found an abundance of material online about that night, including pictures and emails." She also determined that the alleged attackers were boys she had considered friends. Pott then wrote on Facebook that the whole school knew what happened and that her life was ruined. Members of the Pott family recently accused the alleged attackers of destroying evidence in the case, writing on Facebook that the "the boys who we believe responsible for Audrie's death took deliberate steps to destroy evidence and interfere with the police investigation." The family asked students with information about the case to come forward.

Bullycide victim: Andy Cain

Andrew "Andy" Cain, 19, committed suicide after the local Sheriff's Office posted a sarcastic comment about him on Facebook stating they had three warrants out for his arrest when he fatally shot himself in the head in Pullman, Washington. The teen's family is now blaming the Sheriff's Office for Cain's death because, just days before, the following message was posted on its Facebook page: "We have decided that Andrew Cain is no longer the Wanted Person of the Week... he is the Wanted Person of the Month of June. Congratulations!"

Loved ones say Cain was bullied by law enforcement and that the post was "childish." Cain's sister, Alise Smith, told KREM-2 News that the messages became too much for the teen to handle. "Those are the people protecting us, that is just not right," Smith said. "It's like he couldn't escape it for five minutes because everyone around him shared it and was bringing it up."

Smith added that she received a text message from her brother early last week that he felt like putting a bullet through his brain. The text included a screen shot of Facebook messages from the deputy who urged Cain to turn himself in. Smith said she wants an apology from the person who wrote the message, but has yet to receive one. However, Latah County Sheriff Wayne Rausch apologized to the family and said he told the person responsible for the message to not do anything like that ever again. The three warrants out for Cain's arrest had been for driving without privileges and for possession of a controlled substance.

Bullycide victim: Eden Wormer

Eden Wormer, an eighth grader at Cascade Middle School in Vancouver, Washington, hanged herself. The 14-year-old girl whose <u>Facebook</u> page says she loves *"all my haterz"* committed suicide after enduring two years of bullying by her female classmates, her family claims.

The girl's family told ABC-News affiliate KATU that she committed suicide after two years of being bullied by girls in her class. Wormer's older sister, Audri, told the station that Eden changed her appearance several times in an effort to fit in, and begged her older sister not to report the bullying because she thought it would only make the problem worse.

Wormer's Facebook page is a bittersweet mix of "tween" angst where she wrote: *"im super funny and outgoing I love all my friends n family n that includes all my haterz.! ☺n im funn to hang around too. ☺"* In a Feb. 12 post, she wrote: *"omg im such a loner I have a valentine n the only thing im celebrating valentines day with is my bummble bee pillow pet like this iff u have no valentines too or iff u wanna be my valentine. ☺"*

Police in Vancouver say they haven't found evidence that the alleged bullying violated any state laws, according to KATU. Both the school and the Evergreen School District are talking to students and investigating what might have happened and whether any bullying had been documented.

Following her death, Wormer's friends wrote mournful words on her Facebook page. Brook Radtke wrote: *"Eden you are an amazing beautiful person I will miss you forever love isabel and brook."*

Bullycide victim: Phoebe Prince

Phoebe Prince, 15, a recent Irish immigrant, hanged herself after nearly 3 months of routine torment by students at South Hadley High School, via text message, and through the social networking site, Facebook. Prince, a freshman, was reportedly harassed by older girls who resented her dating an older football player. Her death shook the town of South Hadley and prompted the Massachusetts legislature to pass a law introducing an anti-bullying curriculum in the state's public schools.

Nine Massachusetts teenagers were charged in the "unrelenting" bullying of Prince. Two of them were charged with Statutory Rape. Northwestern District Attorney Elizabeth Scheibel said Prince's bullying was the result of a romantic relationship she had with one of the male suspects that ended weeks prior to her suicide. Scheibel called Prince's suicide "the culmination of a nearly three-month campaign of verbally assaulting behavior and threats of physical harm." In at least one instance she was attacked when a girl pelted her with a soft drink can. "The investigation revealed relentless activity directed toward Phoebe, designed to humiliate her and to make it impossible for her to remain at school," Scheibel said. "The bullying, for her, became intolerable." The district attorney said school administrators knew of the bullying but none would be charged; 3 of the 9 teens were indicted on charges connected to Prince's suicide; 3 of the indicted students are girls, charged with Violating Prince's Civil Rights, Criminal Harassment and Disturbing a School Assembly; 2 of the indicted students, a 17-year-old male and an 18-year-old male, were charged with Statutory Rape. Criminal complaints were filed against 3 other students. Of the 6 indicted students, 3 are still students at the school and 3 were expelled.

Bullycide victim: Carolina Picchio

Carolina Picchio, 14, from Novara, Italy, near Milan, had an enviably pretty face and a bright future. Then, late one night, she jumped out of her bedroom window from her family's 4th-floor apartment. She died instantly when she landed headfirst on the pavement below. Before she jumped, she updated her status on <u>Facebook</u> with a chilling suicide note: *"Forgive me if I'm not strong. I cannot take it any longer."*

In her bedroom, police found a note to her ex-boyfriend, whose friends had been circulating a suggestive video of her, taken at a drinking party, in which she appeared tipsy and disheveled. The boys had also been sending her nasty text messages on <u>Facebook</u> with insults and threats. On the day she took her life, she had received 2,600 vulgar messages through Whatsapp. *"Haven't you done enough to me already?"* she wrote in the letter to her former boyfriend. *"How many times do I have to pay?"*

The tables turned when Valentina Sellaroli, an investigating prosecutor in Novara, announced they would press criminal charges against the 8 boys who were "making Picchio pay." The teens, between the ages of 13 and 17, included Picchio's ex-boyfriend. Francesco Saluzzo, another investigating prosecutor, said they were also opening an investigation into whether or not **Facebook** could be held criminally responsible in the young girl's tragic death. **Italy has a precedent for prosecuting Internet crimes. In 2010, three Google Italia executives were given suspended jail terms for failing to remove a video of a group of adolescents bullying a handicapped boy that had been posted in 2006.**

David Voelkert and Angela Voelkert

STUPID HIT MAN #1

Angela Voelkert created a fake profile on <u>Facebook</u> using the name "Jessica Studebaker" with a photo of a sexy teenage girl, to spy on her soon-to-be ex-husband, **David Voelkert**. After conversing with her husband for awhile under his Facebook alias, he confided to Studebaker his plot to have his wife killed, informed the fake teenager that he planted a tracking device on her vehicle so he would know where she was at all times. He then asked the Studebaker if there were any 'thugs' at her school that would do the 'hit' for $10,000. Angela Voelkert then went to the authorities to turn him in.

But Angela's husband was released soon after being taken into custody. He had evidence that he knew it was his wife all along and provided FBI agents with a notarized affidavit in which he describes receiving a Friend request from "Jessica Studebaker," whom he suspected was his ex-wife. "I was lying to this person," he stated, "to gain positive proof that it is indeed my ex-wife trying to again tamper in my life. In no way do I have plans to leave with my children or do any harm to Angela Dawn Voelkert or anyone else." The allegedly incriminating Facebook messages were sent on May 31, six days *after* his sworn affidavit was notarized. Voelkert kept one copy of the affidavit, and gave a relative a second copy for safekeeping. Case closed.

London Eleye and Tim Bynum

STUPID HIT MAN #2

London Eleye, 20, from Pennsylvania, posted a <u>Facebook</u> message on May 23, 2011 seeking a hit-man to kill her 1-year old baby's father. **Tim Bynum,** 18, could win the "Stupidest Facebook Criminal Award" for responding to London publicly on Facebook about the murder-for-hire by requiring the $1,000 be paid to him "up front."

London's "ex" saw the posts and reported it to police. Detectives searched Bynum's apartment and found a 22-caliber handgun with serial number filed off.

London was charged with Murder-for-Hire, and Bynum was charged with Attempted Murder and weapons charge. It doesn't pay to advertise.

2.

PLENTY OF (DEAD) FISH

(POF- PlentyOfFish.com)

Danueal Drayton, Zynea Barney, Samantha Stewart

HE SEEMED NICE

Zynea Barney of Long Island, said she met a "cool guy," **Danueal Drayton**, 27, of New Haven, Connecticut, on the dating app <u>Plenty Of Fish</u> in November 2017. She said he "seemed nice" – a good listener who was interested in her work with the disabled and he had a big vocabulary and ability to fix cars. The couple dated for 6 months without issues before she decided to call off the relationship when he became overly possessive. Then he stalked her, slashed her tires, threatened to cut her brake lines and on June 13, 2017, he tried to strangle her in a park near her but she escaped when factory workers passing by rushed over to help her. Police were called but for reasons that remain unclear, Drayton wasn't arrested. He continued to stalk Barney online and threatened to kill her young son.

Drayton was later arrested in Los Angeles at the residence as a woman who he had tied up and held against her will, and was also charged in a Brooklyn case with Attempted Murder, Imprisonment by Violence, and Sexual Penetration With A Foreign Object. After his arrest, Drayton claimed he murdered 7 women, including **Samantha Stewart,** 29, a nurse from Queens, New York, who was found dead in her apartment on July 17th with all her teeth knocked out, her tongue hanging out and head and neck trauma. He also pled guilty to Raped and Attempted Murder of a 28-year old woman who he held captive in a Hollywood, California apartment and also boasted about killing 6 other women – 2 in Connecticut, one in the Bronx. Drayton allegedly told police to New York, *"My body did this, not my mind. I didn't want to do this. My body made me do this."*

"Things are not always what they seem;
the first appearance deceives many"
-Phaedrus, a Roman poet

John Altinger and Mark Twitchell

COPYCAT KILLER

Mark Andrew Twitchell, 29, from Edmonton, Alberta, Canada, met **John Brian "Johnny" Altinger,** 38, an oil field equipment engineer, on PlentyOfFish.com. On October 10, 2008, Altinger informed his friends he was going to meet a woman with whom he had been chatting online. His friends soon became concerned when they received strange emails from Altinger explaining that he had met a woman who was taking him on a long vacation to Costa Rica and Altinger's boss received a resignation letter by email, but never got a forwarding address requested for Altinger's final paycheck. After becoming more suspicious, Altinger's friends broke into his condo, only to find his passport, dirty dishes, and no indication that he had packed up to leave.

Twitchell was arrested October 31, 2008, charged with First Degree Murder of Altinger on whose laptop police discovered his plan "to become a serial killer." Twitchell was also charged with Attempted Murder for his alleged attack on **Gilles Tetreault** who was lured by Twitchell on Plenty Of Fish with the expectation of meeting a woman, only to be attacked by a masked man with a stun gun when he arrived at the garage rented by Twitchell but Tetreault was able to escape with his life. Twitchell was convicted of murdering and dismembering Altinger. Media dubbed him the "Copycat Killer" because he was inspired by the "Dexter Morgan" character in Jeff Lindsay novels and the "*Dexter*" TV series, about a serial killer.

*"The police, finding a corpse with 28 stab wounds in a bathtub
suspected foul play."*
-Steven Lillebuen, "The Devil's Cinema"

Ingrid Lyne and John Charlton

RED FLAGS MISSED

Ingrid Lyne, 40, a nurse and mother of 3 girls, met **John Robert Charlton**, 37, met on Plenty Of Fish They had been dating long-distance for about a month when Lyne went missing after they came home after attending the Mariners' home opener game on April 8, 2016.

Charlton claimed he was so drunk he didn't know how they got back to Lyne's home in Renton, Washington, nor what happened that night and woke up on a sidewalk the next morning. He said he believed he and Lyne had sex but that Lyne was "acting weird" and he could provide no further details during his police interview when detectives observed an abrasion to his forehead, injuries to his lip and chin, scratches on his chest and an abrasion on his left hand. Charlton had a record of Domestic Violence Assault and a DUI in Auburn, Washington in 1998, a 2006 conviction for Aggravated Robbery in Utah, and a 2009 conviction for Felony Theft in Montana. His parents, Ray and JoAnn Charlton, filed for a Restraining Order when he tried to provoke a fight with them while drunk and abusive and felt he was becoming mentally unstable.

The body of Ingrid Lyne was found "in pieces" in a Seattle, Washington, recycling bin. A 15-inch pruning saw was near her bathtub and blood was on her car seat. Charlton was charged with First Degree Murder and Theft of Lyne's car which was found in Seattle. He allegedly killed the victim, dismembered her body, and drove to Seattle where he discarded her remains. He was sentenced to 28 Years in Prison. The prosecutor commented *"We may never understand why she was killed."*

Katie Locke and Carl Langdell

THE MOTIVE WAS SEX

Carl Langdell, 26, was given a minimum sentence of 26 years after confessing to strangling to death **Katie Locke,** 23, a teacher, and sexually assaulting her corpse. He killed her on their first and only date resulting from their contact via <u>Plenty Of Fish</u>, on Christmas eve, 2015, in a hotel room in East London.

Landell, who lied in is POF profile that he was a lawyer with his own law firm, had previously been diagnosed with Emotionally Unstable Personality Disorder and had been discharged from a psychiatric unite just 2 months before he killed Katie. And months before the murder, Langdell had avoided prison and got a suspended sentence after making threats to kill a community nurse, which he claimed was just an attempt to shock mental health officials to get their attention. He had told a mental health worker that he had fantasies of cutting a girl's throat, seeing her naked and having sex with her dead body – That was 9 months before the murder. After the murder, he claimed he had killed Ms. Locke in a sex game. Former boyfriends of Locke confirmed she had previously shown no interest in anything other than "conventional" sex.

Langdell was arrested near the canal in Lea Valley Park which is when he told an officer Katie's body was 10 metres from a skip on the grounds of the hotel. He would not answer further questions, but a forensic analysis indicated his use of cocaine, diazepam and drugs used in the treatment of depression and anxiety.

Adam Hilarie, Hailey Bustos   Andre Warner, Gary Gray, Joshua Ellington

"In a world of thieves,
the only final sin is stupidity."
-Hunter S. Thompson

THE MOTIVE WAS MONEY

Hailey Rose Bustos, 18, and 3 men, were charged with the Murder in the death of **Adam Hilarie, 27**, who she met on a date via <u>PlentyOfFish</u>, which bills itself as the largest date site in the world.

There was no reason for Adam Hilarie to believe anything but the obvious: He had been on a promising first date with a pretty girl. He had picked her up and they went bowling in Winter Haven Florida at Cypress Lanes, which offers shoe and lane rentals for a quarter on Thursday nights, and specials on pizza and beer. A few hours later, the pair ended up at his place, where they talked a bit more and met up with his roommate. Then Hilarie dropped his date off at her home.

Afterward, Bustos sent the single father a text: She'd had a good time and wanted to meet up the following night at his place. The next night, her real intentions became clear. Bustos brought three men with her to Hilarie's place, including two career criminals on probation for violent felonies. At least one of the men, police said, had a gun. When Hilarie responded to the knock on his door, the men overpowered him and dashed inside. The struggle ended in the kitchen. Hilarie was begging for his life, not putting up any kind of fight, and was telling them that he had a 5-year old daughter. Hilarie was shot in the head and collapsed on the kitchen floor. As Hilarie bled out, the suspects pulled their car to the front of the apartment and began stealing the dead man's Xbox, iPhone and TVs that Bustos had spotted the night before. For her role in the deadly robbery, *she was paid $50.*

Marty McMillan Jr. and John McRae

THE MOTIVE WAS JEALOUSY

John McRae, 40, of Southeast D.C., was charged with Second Degree Murder in the death of **Marty McMillan Jr.,** 22, of Landover, Maryland. It all began with late night communications over <u>Plenty Of Fish</u> on April22, 2017, and ended with gunshots into a bedroom closet where McMillan had been hiding.

McMillan's family told investigators that Marty had been communicating on the date site with a woman who had the user name "Luv 33" who was later identified in court documents as "W-3." W-3 and another woman were both living together with and in a 3-way relationship with McRae, when W-3 (aka "Luv 33") also invited McMillan over while McRae was at work, and Marty engaged in sex with her. But when McRae came home early at 2 am, McMillan hid is a closet. McRae figured out that a man was there and W-3 ran from the room as McRae grabbed a gun and fired shots into the closet.

*"He'd kill you all right, no sweat.
But for all the wrong reasons.
Amateurs' reasons, of course,
But you'll be just as dead."*
-Laurell K. Hamilton,
"The Laughing Corpse"

Ranee McKelvey and David Reid

THE MOTIVE WAS MURDER

David Reid, 47, of Flint, Michigan, while on parole stemming from an assault, moved into the home of **Renee Marie McKelvey**, 53, in Grand Blanc Township, Michigan, after meeting her on <u>Plenty Of Fish</u>. The arrangement didn't last long.

McKelvey was found lying face down on her bed, dead from manual suffocation. The natural gas line behind the stove had been turned on, the house was filled with gas, and there were candles burning, but no fire resulted to cover up the murder.

Reid was charged on Valentine's Day, February 14, 2018, with Murder and Attempted Arson.

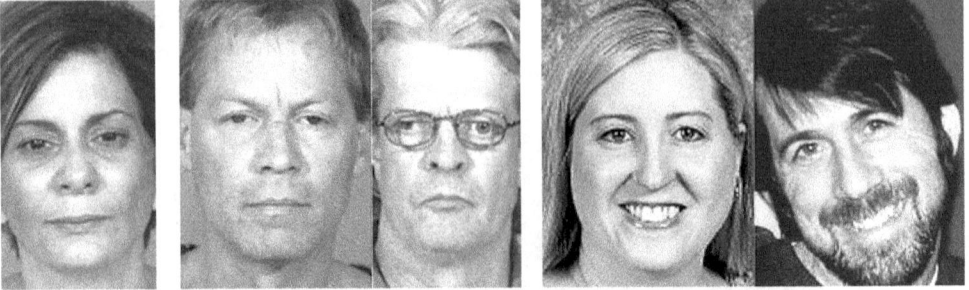
Monserrate Shirley - Mark & Robert Leonard - Jennifer & "Dion" Longworth

A PLAN THAT WENT TERRIBLY WRONG

Monserrate ("Moncy") Shirley, 50, survived her horrific childhood of abuse inflicted by her father, earned a nursing degree, and was working in a hospital's intensive care unit. **Mark Leonard,** 42, made his living by preying on innocent women on date sites, and taking their money. One woman won a $70,000 judgment against Leonard in a civil suit after lending him $53,000, which he never repaid.

Leonard was again broke when he found "Moncy" via Plenty of Fish and moved into her home in Indianapolis. But Moncy, too, was in debt. So he convinced her to increase insurance coverage on her home to $300,000 and allow him to start a fire for which he hired his half-brother, **Robert Leonard, Jr.,** 56, to do the job so they could collect on the insurance. Leonard and Shirley first removed their items of value from the house, then were seen on a casino's surveillance cameras endlessly wandering but never gambling, on November 10, 2012 when, instead of starting a fire in the garage, Robert Leonard rigged the timer on the microwave so it would spark after he opened the natural gas. Instead of a house fire, the house exploded, destroying 80 neighboring homes were damaged or destroyed from the explosion and ensuing flames. **John "Dion"** and **Jennifer Longworth** were both killed in the fires; 7 others were injured. Not finding any of Shirley's possessions of value in the rubble, investigators put all the suspicious pieces together. Mark Leonard was sentenced to 75 Years Plus 2 Life Sentences. On January 20, 2018, Mark Leonard died in prison of natural causes at age 48. Robert Leonard, who caused the explosion, was sentenced for Felony Murder to Life Without Parole. Monserrate Shirley pled guilty to Arson and Conspiracy and was sentenced to 50 Years with earliest December 19, 2037 when she will be 72.

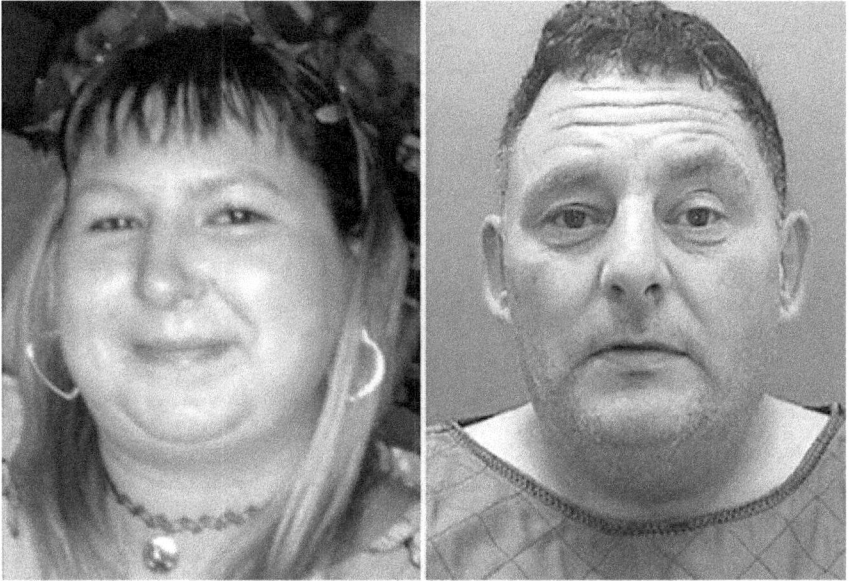

Katherine Smith and Anthony Lowe

JUST PRACTICING

Would-be serial killer, **Anthony Lowe,** 46, whose screen name was Tony Moore on <u>Plenty Of Fish</u>, was also approaching several women on <u>Facebook</u> the day after he murdered **Katherine Smith**, 26, who he had stabbed 33 times. The murder occurred in Ely, Cardiff (Wales), less than 8 weeks after Smith and Lowe first connected via Plenty Of Fish.

When he contacted his next potential victim, she asked *"I thought you were in a relationship?"* to which he replied, *"No, I am single now."*

3.
MURDEROUS
MATCHES

"I beg you don't say goodbye
Can't we give our love another try?
C'mon baby, let's start anew,
'Cause breaking up is hard to do."
-song written and performed by Sedaka
with Howard Greenfield,
1962 and 1975

Anne Simenson, Mary Kay Beckman, Wade Ridley

LONG DISTANCE RELATIONSHIPS
NEVER WORK

Wade Ridley, 53, of Las Vegas, was so pissed at **Anne Simonsen**, 62, of Phoenix, for breaking off their relationship THAT resulted from meeting via Match.com, that, on January 21, 2011, he drove to her Phoenix home where he brutally beat, stomped on her head and neck 8 times, and stabbed her 10 times with a machete and a butcher knife, "until she stopped making the gurgling noise." He then stole her car, along with her jewelry and electronics. When he was pulled over driving Simonson's car and arrested outside the Hard Rock Hotel.

Incredibly, Simonson survived the attack, although she was in critical condition and underwent several surgeries to repair her jaw, save her eyesight and hearing, and to replace part of her skull.

Ridley was charged with Attempted Murder of Simonson in Arizona and also the murder another ex-girlfriend, **Mary Kay Beckman**, 49.

BECKMAN v. MATCH.com

Then, in 2013, Mary Kay Beckman sued Match.com for $10-million, citing negligence, negligent misrepresentation, deceptive trade, failure to warn and negligent infliction of emotional distress, seeking $346,000 in economic damages, $5.4-million in non-economic damages, and $4.1 million in punitive damages.

She claimed that the site led her to believe that she'd end up in a "stable and loving relationship with another member" and didn't properly warn her about the dangers of meeting "an individual whose intentions are not to find a mate, but to find victims to kill or rape."

In a statement, Match.com agreed that what happened to Beckman was "horrible" but said that the lawsuit was "absurd" and that the site cannot be held responsible for the actions of one "sick, twisted individual." However, Beckman never got to sue Ridley himself. Ridley had since committed suicide in prison after being convicted of assaulting Beckman (he was also wanted for allegedly murdering an ex-girlfriend whom Beckman says Ridley also met through Match.com)

In 2016, the Ninth Circuit remanded Beckman's "duty to warn" claim against Match.com to a lower court, saying she should have a chance to prove that Match.com *knew* Ridley had been paired with, and attacked, other women using its platform. The lower court dismissed the claim in 2017, finding Match *doesn't* owe a duty to *"control the dangerous conduct of another or to warn others of the dangerous conduct, except where a special relationship exists and the harm is created by foreseeable conduct."* The case was finally dismissed at the Ninth Circuit Court of Appeals at San Francisco (Mary Kay Beckman v. Match.com, No. 13-16324 filed 9-1-16) when it was argued that "To impose a duty to warn in that circumstance really opens up Match to a plethora of liability and a duty to investigate, a duty to look into things over which it really has no control. This could create a cost-free way to harm people online." The rebuttal suggested "It wouldn't take much for Match to issue a standard warning about complaints against certain users in a way that would protect privacy. "An individual warning to the email, perhaps automatically generated, that could put this person on notice and use give these individuals an opportunity to protect themselves... Match is in control of the information. Match is in a superior position to help other people make good conscious decisions and they are choosing to not do that."

"Rape is like being murdered but still being alive."
-Home Office 2010,
cited in Stern Review 2010,
ScienceDirect.com

Jason Lawrence

SERIAL RAPISTS WELCOME

Jason Lawrence, 50, a married father of 3 children from his first marriage, was found guilty of raping 5 women who he met on Match.com and chatted to 3,000 potential victims in 2014-2015. He overpowered 7 women at hotels, homes and a makeshift bed in his van; 3 were raped after he married his 2nd wife, Sara White, 52, who he also met on Match.com; she was not a victim but has since dumped him; 4 victims complained to Match.com_but it refused to bar him *"because he had not posted offensive or abusive comments online."*

Police believe there may have been other victims who have not come forward. The attacks were carried out in the Midlands and East of England. One victim, raped in St. Ives, said *"I don't understand how someone can go from being so nice to some kind of monster within an hour."* Lawrence claimed the encounters were consensual and he was only caught when his final known victim went to police and they discovered the unreported attacks.

*They were all damaged goods. basically.
Their needs were such that they couldn't really find satisfaction
or get their needs met in a normal healthy relationship.
They had to find love behind the prison walls.*"
-Taylor Bell, "Women Who Love Men Behind Bars"

James Holmes

VISITING HOURS FOR KILLER'S MATCH DATES

James Eagan Holmes, at age 25, was "the Aurora Movie Theater Massacre Shooter" that killed 12 people and injured 70 others during the showing of the movie, *"The Dark Knight Rises"* on July 20, 2012. Holmes said if he had not been captured, he would "kill again." Holmes posted an eerie profile headline on <u>Match.com,</u> 6 days prior to the shooting, that said *"Will You Visit Me in Prison?"* In August 2015, Holmes received 12 Life Sentences Plus 3,318 Years. Among the photos released by media were several creepy selfies, his Match.com profile, and photos that hang in his jail cell of women who Holmes claims are *still obsessed with him.*

His Match.com profile indicated he was looking for "women ages 19 to 38 for flings, foodies, activity partners or whatevs" and he told viewers to message him if they're looking for "sexy times."

4.

tinder
trap

*"Nobody owns life
but anyone who can pick up a frying pan owns death."*
-William S. Borroughs

Jaqueline Vandergriff and Charles Bryant

SUSPICIONS CONFIRMED

Jaqueline "Jackie" Vandergriff, 24, a licensed esthetician, was also a Texas Woman's University (TWU) student studying nutrition, and a part-time waitress. **Charles Dean Bryant**, 30, had worked at a bar and a fitness gym had been let go due to attendance issues and had previously been arrested and accused of Criminal Trespassing and Stalking in Denton County, posted bond, and was released from jail September 9th. The night Vandergriff disappeared, she tweeted that she had been talking with a guy on Tinder who she suspected of using a fake account to attract her interest. *Still,* she met Bryant the first time in person *that same night* at the Urban Cowboy Saloon, the largest gay club in Fort Worth. Security camera footage shows them together, leaving Fry Street Public House, and walking down the street to Shots and Crafts.

It was only after firefighters put out a fire in Acorn Woods Park that authorities found Vanderfriff's dismembered body, identified by her fingerprints. Cell phone tower data last placed her near Bryant's home in Haslet on September 13, 2016. Bryant was then arrested. He admitted dismembering her body, but claimed it was an accidental death from hitting her head against the interior of his car, and accidental asphyxiation after he placed a zip-tie around her neck during consensual sex. But at Bryant's trial, both the Defense and Prosecution conceded that he went to Walmart and bought a shovel early in the morning of September 14th, intent on burying Vandergriff's body. Guns, knives and a saw were found at Bryant's apartment. Bryant was found Guilty of Murder and got a Life sentence.

Sydney Loofe, Aubrey Trail, Bailey Boswell

OUT OF CHARACTER

Sydney Loofe, 24, of Lincoln, Nebraska, was looking forward to meeting, **Bailey Boswell**, 23, a woman with whom she connected through the Tinder dating app. After getting dressed and applying her makeup, she posted a selfie on Snapchat captioned *"Ready for my date"* who she called her *"dream girl."* Snaps from that evening showed Loofe and Boswell enjoying a night out on the town together, in Wilbur, where they were seen together by numerous witnesses. Loofe even contacted a friend about how successfully the date had gone and her plans to go on another date with Boswell.

The following day, Sidney neglected to show up at her job as a cashier at Menard's Home Improvement and hadn't called in sick, which was "out of character" for her. Her worried parents filed a missing persons report. For 3 weeks, Sydney's car sat untouched in the driveway of her apartment. Then, in early December 2017, her body was discovered on farm land in a rural part of Edgar in Clay County. Most of her internal organs were gone, including her tongue, kidney, and heart. They knew it was Loofe, from a tattoo on her arm. Boswell had been arrested on unrelated charges just 6 days before Loofe's body was recovered. But in January 2018, **Aubrey Trail** confessed to the murder of Sydney Loofe. He claimed that, on November 16, he accidentally suffocated her during a group sex session that involved 2 other individuals, that she had something wrapped around her neck at the time, and that he dismembered her out of panic.

Friends who knew her sexual preference as a lesbian doubted that she would have *consented* to intimacy with a *man*.

66

"I'm thinking' he remarked quietly,
'whether I shall add to the disorder of this room
by scattering your brains across the fine place."
-Wilkie Collins, "The Woman In White"

Gable Tostee and Warriena Wright

GETTING AWAY WITH MURDER

Warriena Wright, 26, of New Zealand, and **Gable Tostee**, 28, Australian born and with a troubled past, met on <u>Tinder</u>. They then met for drinks one night at 8.45 pm. By 2:21 am, Warriena Wright was dead.

Tostee's decision to secretly *record* their date inside his apartment an hour before Wright's fatal fall from his 14th floor apartment was key evidence at Tostee's trial. After having sex, the pair had a violent drunken fight. It was argued that Tostee had physically restrained and restricted Wright's throat with his forearm and was recorded telling her, just prior to his locking her outside on his balcony: *"If you try and pull anything, I'll knock you out. I'll knock you the f−k out. Do you understand?... You're lucky I haven't chucked you off my balcony you goddamn psycho little bitch. I'm gonna walk you about of this apartment just the way you are, you're not going to collect any belongings."* His defense attorney said Tostee's intimidating conduct left Wright feeling she had no means of escape, other than scaling the balcony. She screamed *"No!"* 33 times in 45 seconds, then twice said *"I want to go home."* Her scream was heard as she fell to her death. Her voice proved she was so fearful that she tried to climb down to the balcony below but fell to her death. Tostee first phoned his lawyer, rather than first calling 000 (U.K.'s "911").

The court acquitted Gable Tostee of either Murder or Manslaughter in the death of Warriena Wright just hours after defense lawyers had called for a mistrial.

Emmanuel Bocangegra and Francia Ibarra

SHE JUST SAID NO.

Francia Ruth Ibarra's <u>Tinder</u> date didn't go well. Ibarra, 26, was last seen with **Emmanuel Delani Valdez Bocangegra,** 26, before her parents of Leon, Central Mexico City, reported her missing, and then her bag and some of her clothes were found in his apartment. Then human bones were discovered in garbage bags beside caustic soda and hydrochloric acid on his apartment balcony. The remains were of Francia Ibarra.

Authorities believe Bocangegra, an ex-medical student, through the dating app, Tinder, and met up with him several times in the months before her December 3, 2016 disappearance.

Authorities believe Bocangegra, who was emotionless upon capture, had murdered and dissolved Ibarra's body in acid... because she refused to have sex with him.

Joshua Stimpson and Molly McLaren

WALKING ON EGGS

Molly McLaren, 23, met **Joshua Stimpson,** 26, on <u>Tinder</u> in July 2016 and they began a relationship during which they reportedly had been having problems. McLaren described Stimpson's behavior as "childish, "pathetic," "manipulative," and "really nasty and threatening." She felt she was *"constantly treading on eggshells around him"* and was worried that he would keep turning up at her house in Kent (U.K.).

On June 17, 2017, she broke up with him. The next day, he was angry and posted derogatory, false comments about her, alleging she was taking drugs. She told friends *"I'm actually scared of what he might do to me."* On June 22, a North Kent police officer phoned Stimpson on speakerphone in McLaren's presence and said to him *"We wouldn't want Molly to come to the police station about you again, would we?"* Stimpson replied, *"Wouldn't we?"*

On June 29, 2017, McLaren didn't notice Stimpson rushing toward her until he yanked her car door open in her gym's parking lot. A witness heard McLaren screaming, trying to pull him off her as he stabbed her **75 times** in a frenzy. The bystander tried to stop him by slamming the car door on Stimpson's leg. McLaren stopped screaming when he cut her throat. Covered in blood, Stimpson walked toward the approaching police car and said ""*You want me*" before being arrested as the scene. But in a plea deal, Stimpson pled guilty to Manslaughter of Molly McLaren, based on the claim that Stimpson was suffering from "diminished responsibility." Still, he was sentenced to a well-deserved 26 Years-to-Life in prison.

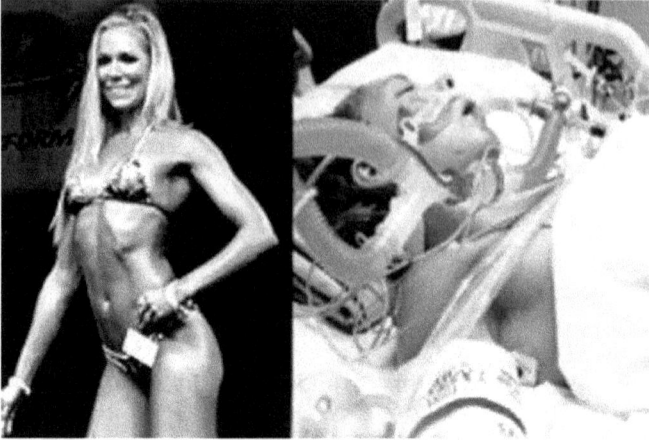

Korren Knapp-Grada

WORSE THAN DEATH

On May 29, 2017, Korren Knapp-Grada, then 29, made contact with a man on Tinder who called himself "John" and agreed to meet him at a San Diego bar in the Gaslight Quarter. But the last thing she recalls is that he ordered her a drink. Tests would show she had been given a "date rape" drug.

The next morning, Memorial Day, May 30, 2017, she was being struck by 2 hit-and-run drivers on Interstate 8, near the Viejas Casino. A semi-truck driver had come to her rescue, dragged Korren off the freeway to safety, and kept her breathing while awaiting paramedics. Two weeks later, she woke up in a coma at a hospital ICU suffering from horrific, painful, life-threatening injuries, with her right leg mangled, her pelvis crushed and her bladder lacerated. She underwent 20 surgeries within the year following that deadly Tinder date, has had several severe complications since, and there are still more surgeries ahead. Originally from New York, before that fateful night, she was a bodybuilder, NPC bikini athlete/model and fitness enthusiast who worked as a tattoo apprentice and had been a senior art director at advertising agencies. She said *"I had my belongings on one side of 9-foot fence and I had jumped over it. I think I was trying to get help. I think he (the man from the bar) was trying to rape me or something... I believe, and my doctors have also noted, that my muscle mass at the time was likely one of the reasons I survived it."*

Kaitlin Hurley and Officer Lee Martin-Cramp

A VICTIM'S LIFE SENTENCE

Kaitlin Hurley was studying nursing at University of Health Sciences, Antigua, when she connected on <u>Tinder</u> with London Police Officer **Lee Martin-Cramp,** 26 , who was staying at the Pineapple Resort in Antigua for a wedding with friends and family. On May 23, 2015, they met in Antigua at a dockside boat party. According to their texts and later testimony, she agreed to meet him on condition that there would be no sex involved as she was a devout Christian and wished to remain virgin until marriage. They shared a bottle of wine and had opened a second bottle before returning to Hurley's apartment so she could change her clothes. She said she didn't like the taste of the second wine and felt dizzy. Martin-Cramp told her he had added Vodka to her drink when actually he had slipped her a "date rape drug." She remembers screaming, telling him "no" and to "stop" yet found herself naked in bed with him the next morning and with a bite mark on her neck and several bruises. A medical exam confirmed she had been raped.

His lawyer "blamed the victim" claiming her consumption of alcohol and inviting him into her home suggests she consented. Hurley completed her degree in Antigua but now distrusts humanity and gave up her dream of being a missionary nurse. Said Hurley *"If you can't trust a police officer, who can you trust?"* Martin-Cramp was sentenced to 15 years in prison with credit for time served. The rape victim got a life sentence.

5.

CUPID
KILLERS
(OKCupid.com)

*"Men should think twice about making widowhood
women's only path to power,"*
-Gloria Steinem

Charles Billis, Kevin Leland

Christine Billis

THE OKCUPID KILLER

NBC and other media called her "The OKCupid Killer." **Christine Billis** of Vermont was 44 when she was arrested on a charge of First Degree Murder, in June 2011, in the 2009 death of her husband, **Charles Billis,** which was downgraded in a plea deal to Manslaughter due to ambiguities in the case that might make "Murder" hard to prove. But she might have got away with it if she hadn't confided in her OKCupid date, **Kevin Leland**, in August 2010, that she had killed her husband.

In 2009, police, at first, thought the car crash on Route 5A in Charleston was the result of her husband having a medical episode when he swerved into a tree. But in 2011, she told Leland, *"I killed him. I drove him into the tree on purpose."* She was wearing a seatbelt; he was not. Leland secretly *recorded* their conversations. Billis claimed her husband was controlling and abusive, a claim that was not addressed in court. She was sentenced to 7-to-15 Years in Prison, which prosecutors termed "reasonable for this woman who almost got away with murder."

It could have become 2 murders – According to Leland, "After only knowing her maybe 2 or 3 weeks, texting and phone calls, she confessed to me very remorsefully that she killed her husband" But also "She threatened to kill me if I recorded her and turned her in. There was one time she stood right over me with a knife, looking at this hunting knife, a 13-inch blade… it was sketchy, and she has a lot of sketchy friends, some of them that are threatening me now." He said it remains a mystery why she trusted him with her secrets.

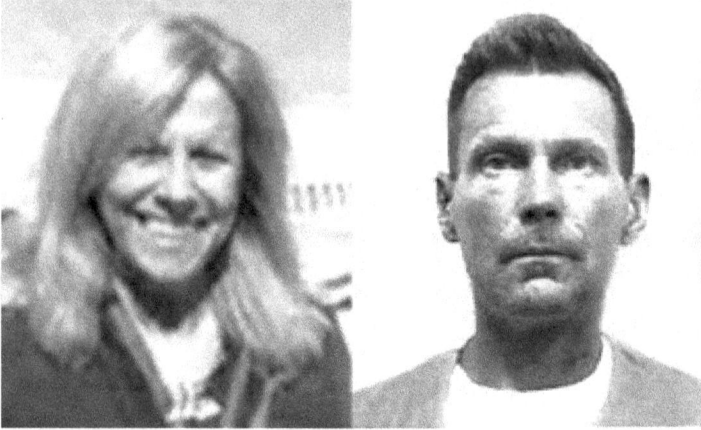

Lorraine Long and Robert Wiesner

LOVE KILLS

Lorraine Pauline Long, 62, from Scottsdale, Arizona, finding herself alone for the first time in many years following the death of her husband, decided to try OKCupid, an online date site that claims to set up 30,000 dates every single day. That's how she met **Robert Wiesner,** 52, also from Scottsdale, who swept her off her feet. But things quickly took a turn for the worse when Long had to file a restraining order against Wiesner, which may have pushed Wiesner over the edge.

Authorities said he shot Long to death on August 6, 2010, after driving her, against her will, from Phoenix to home she owned in a remote area of Seligman Verde Ranch in Seligman, Arizona, and that an argument escalated during the drive. Wiesner was transported to Flagstaff Medical Center with a non-life threatening gunshot wound, while Long was pronounced dead at the same hospital. Weisner was arrested on August 7, 2010. In his Death Penalty Murder case, Wiesner was accused of First Degree Murder, Kidnapping, Burglary, Aggravated Harassment and Sexual Assault. But in May, 2015, to avoid the Death Penalty, he accepted a plea deal and was found guilty of Second Degree Murder and Second Degree Burglary and was sentenced to 27 Years in Prison

*"Killing is killing, whether done
for duty, profit or fun."*
-Richard Ramirez, "The Night Stalker"

Charlotte Brown and Jack Shepherd

SPEED KILLS

Charlotte "Charlie" Brown, 23, from Essex, East London, England, met **Jack Shepherd**, 30, a British man, on the OKCupid website and on December 8, 2015, took her on a "glamorous date." The date began with a £150 (US $195) meal in The Shard, London's tallest skyscraper, where he offered to take her on his speedboat. He drove Brown in his boat 13 miles along the chilly Thames River. Neither had wetsuits nor life jackets and both had been drinking. Shepherd then handed control to Brown who he said flipped the boat after hitting a submerged log. Shepherd was saved by rescue crews who spotted him hanging from the boat. Brown was unresponsive and died "from cold water immersion."

After the crash, Shepherd left the country in March 2018 and fled 2000 miles away to Georgia, on Russia's border, to avoid prison. After several months on the run, he turned himself in to police in Tbilsi, Georgia, and was extradited back to England. He told police he bought the boat to impress women and his memory of the event was "hazy" as they had both consumed alcohol that night. A woman Shepherd dated before Brown said he had taken her on his boat and she took herself home by taxi as she was uncomfortable with how he was speeding, just as mobile phone video footage showed Brown shouting about his speed which was more than 24 knots - more than twice the speed limit. An investigator stated *"To take his boat out at night, while drinking, in winter conditions and without offering Charlotte a life jacket or even asking if she could swim, was a recipe for disaster.* On January 27, 2018, Shepherd pled "Not Guilty" but the jury, found him Guilty of Manslaughter; he was sentenced to 6 Years in Prison for Manslaughter by Gross Negligence.

6.

deadly
disharmony

(eharmony.com)

*"Serial Killers have a heart
but it's usually someone else's."*
-Anthony T. Hicks

Pamela Butler, Marta Rodriguez   Jose Rodriguez-Cruz

THE VALENTINE KILLER

Pamela J. Butler, 47, of Washington, D.C., met **Jose Angel Rodriguez Cruz**, 51, of Dumfires, Virginia, via eHarmony and they had been in a relationship for 5 months until Butler went missing on Valentine's Day, February 14, 2009. Rodrigues was an ex-military service member suffering from PTSD. Butler, a pretty computer systems analyst at the Environmental Protection Agency, vanished from her home on Valentine's Day, February 14, 2009, after telling her mother that Rodriguez was taking her out for dinner for Valentine's Day.

Thirty years earlier, **Marta Haydee Rodriguez**, 28, a Jose Rodriguez' ex-wife who was a nurse's aide, disappeared in 1989. Before her disappearance, Marta had told police that her estranged husband had assaulted and kidnapped her. Court records contained his statement *"If I can't have her no one will."* Butler's disappearance baffled police because she was last seen on her security video surveillance tape entering her home with Rodriguez, but the footage never captured her leaving. But he was seen on camera entering and exiting her home, taking items out. The one window not covered by her security camera was unlocked and the home was in disarray which was unlike Butler, and her bed sheets were gone. When first questioned, Rodriguez said their relationship ended on February 13th. Rodrigues was arrested 8 years later, April 7, 2017 in D.C., pled guilty to Second Degree Murder, and received a 12 year sentence. As a condition of the plea bargain, he led investigators to Butler's remains found along the I-95. Marta was also buried close to Pamela on the I-95 but her remains were not recoverable and he was not charged with her murder.

"If you are obsessed with someone,
why would you kill her?"
-A. Yazawa

Terrence Black and Susan Loper

HE WAS NO EVIL KNIEVEL

Susan Miller Lopez, 40, a pilates/fitness instructor, was looking for love on eHarmony through which she first met her former boyfriend, **Terrence Black,** 50, of Frisco, Texas, with whom she broke up in 2009. She next met Jason Hayes, in February 2010. When Loper and Hayes broke up, a text message from Loper to her friend, March 2011, stated *"Looks like I will be rejoining eHarmony real soon... I am back on the market. We will have to swap stories from the good and bad matches."* On April 19, 2011, Loper was dead.

Loper's blood stained car was found the night before her body was found in a field along the North Dallas Tollway in Frisco, Texas. She died of multiple blows to the head that caved in her skull and she had been savagely beaten. DNA consistent with Terrence Black, and also Hayes, as well as that of an unknown individual, was found on the gearshift and headrest of Loper's car. DNA found on Loper's shirt was not consistent with *either* Black or Hayes. However, Loper's car , which police believed was used to take her to the field, was shown exiting the Dallas North Tollway at 6:38 a.m. that day in Plano, while Hayes' alibi of being at a doctor's office in Johnson County where he was selling pharmaceuticals at 8:00 a.m. on the day of Loper's death checked out. Hayes' computer had photos of Loper with Hayes that suggested Black had been stalking Loper *after* their breakup. Black was fleeing Park Rangers when *he jumped into the Grand Canyon*, sustaining serious injuries, but survived, was arrested, tried, and found guilty of Capital Murder, and was sentenced to Life Without Parole.

7

with **Death**

(Jdate.com)

JEWISH TRIANGLE

Harry Carlip, 71, met **Marilyn Spiegel,** 69, on JDate, an online dating website geared toward connecting Jewish singles, and sparks were obvious from the start. In fact, they planned to marry aboard the couple's boat at the Salty Sam's Marina on Fort Meyers Beach, Florida.

Two days before their wedding, on May 15, 2015, witnesses saw Marilyn Spiegel's ex-husband, **Michael Spiegel**, 72, board the boat, and then heard Marilyn Spiegel start to scream, which could be heard in a chilling 911 call, as she kept begging her ex-husband to stop. Michael Spiegel stabbed his ex-wife 10 times and shot her fiancé 4 times, then lit the vessel on fire. Spiegel them plodded away from the murder scene "as calm as can be like it was a walk in the park because is plan had been executed." Michael Spiegel had decided if he couldn't have Marilyn, no one would. He was convicted in August 2015 of 2 counts of Second Degree Murder and one count of Arson.

The day before he was to be sentenced, Michael Spiegel jumped to his death from the second floor landing of his cell block at the Lee County Florida Jail Core Facility.

"Where there's a will
there's a potential murder."
-Brahms Lewis

Shele Colvin and Rod Colvin

JDATE JUGGLER TURNED KILLER

Shele Danishefsky, a successful UBS wealth manager, and **Rod Colvin,** a failed stockbroker, met at a Jewish singles event in 1998 and married with in weeks of that meeting despite that she was 11 years older. Rather than pursue his own career, Colvin preferred to live off his wife while compulsively pursuing other women online, as a pro backgammon player. He contacted 50 to 100 women on JDate and Facebook in a single day and using the screen name "James Early" on JDate, juggling more than a dozen lovers at a time, when his wife refused to have an "open" marriage.

The final straw for her was when he came home at 6 a.m. reeking of another woman's perfume. They separated and Colvin moved to a small apartment. In May 2009, she changed locks on her apartment door, obtained a court order of protection, then served him with divorce papers; When he realized he would lose the steady flow of his wife's money, he became violent, choking her during an argument while screaming *"I'll f—king kill you."* Just 2 days before he actually did kill her her, she had emailed her lawyer about cutting him out of her will – a message which he likely intercepted.

Colvin then attempted to frame his 9-year old daughter for the murder while siphoning $80,000 from his kids' college fund. His own parents, David and Carol Colvin, obtained custody of the kids in 2012 and a restraining order against him, which only incensed him. In 2015, Colvin was arrested for his wife's murder, just before he could carry out his plan to kill his parents also, and just 2 months before he was set to inherit at least $1.6-million of his dead wife's $5.2-million fortune.

8.

--for murder

(MeetMe.com)

Leigh Swanson and Steven Fabi

SHE HAD A BAD FEELING

Leigh Swanson, 45, met **Steven Michael Fabi,** 30, on MeetMe.com, while he also had 900 Facebook Friends. On November 16, 2012, just before Swanson went on a blind date with Fabi, Swanson told her mother that she *"had a bad feeling"* about going on the date. Her mother said *"Then don't go."*

But Swanson went on the blind date with him. On November 18, she called her mother from Fabi's home to assure her mom that *"everything is OK"* and that was the last anyone heard from her.

In early December 2012, Swanson's body was found in the Michigan woods near the Sanford area house where Fabi lived with his family. As two deputies arrived at Fabi's home to question him as prime suspect, they heard a loud "boom." Fabi's father ran out of the house telling the deputies *"My son just shot himself!"*

Ashley Pegram and Edward Bonilla

A ONE-TIME THING

Ashley Nicole Pegram, 28, mother of 3 small children, connected with **Edward Bonilla**, 30, via MeetMe.com. Pegram began instant messaging with Bonilla via the MeetMe.com "Kik"app on a cell phone Pegram shared with her sister, **Brandy Chance**, and went on a date with Bonilla on April 3, 2015. When she didn't return home from the date, Chance called Bonita who alleged that Pegram was heavily intoxicated and that he couldn't handle her so kicked her out of his car around midnight on Main Street.

More than a month after her family reported her missing, Pegram's decomposed remains, wearing only a bra, were found by cadaver dogs in a shallow grave at a wooded area near Harleyville, South Carolina. Bonilla's work van showed blood evidence on its ceiling and his stories were inconsistent. Bonita later claimed he accidentally hit her with his Mom's car when she got out to use a restroom; after that, he changed his story claiming she became irate and violent and when he was restraining her to keep her from kicking his car, he accidentally choked her and she died in his arms.

Bonilla was convicted of Murder and sentenced to 30 Years to Life in Prison. His motive is unknown.

Jessica Frank and Erick Joaquin-Espinosa

REJECTION HURT THE REJECTER MORE

Jessica Frank, 19, met **Erick Joaquin-Espinosa,** 23, 3 weeks before her death, through MeetMe.com. Joaquin-Espinosa claimed to Eugene investigators that he killed Frank after the teen told him she loved him and he told her the relationship was moving too quickly for him, so asked her to leave his one-bedroom outbuilding where he lived on his boss' property in North Eugene. He claimed she then threatened to kill him and that he claimed she took a knife and stabbed him in the hand and neck, that he wrestled the knife away from her, and stabbed her in the neck and chest, killing her. Espinosa was observed to have only a small cut, like a paper cut, on his right little finger.

A co-worker of Joaquin-Espinosa, a roofer, gave police a different account. He said he had been in the outbuilding watching a movie with the couple when he fell asleep on a small bed in the room and that he woke to hear an argument between Joaquin-Espinosa and Frank, who were sitting on Joaquin-Espinosa's bed, but didn't understand what they were saying because he doesn't understand English. But he saw Joaquin-Espinosa get up and get a knife and stab Frank several times. The co-worker ran back to his trailer where he lived on their boss' property. Joaquin-Espinosa came to the trailer, took a shower, both men went to sleep, got up next morning and went to work. The co-worker told his boss he had headache and asked to be taken home. That's when the co-worker told his boss about the murder. Investigators found Frank's body in a shallow grave under the floorboard, wrapped in black plastic and a telephone cord.

*"Hell has three gates –
lust, anger, and greed."*
-Bhagavad Gita

Marissa Randall and Soi Dang

SEX, MONEY, AND MURDER

Marissa Randall, who media reported was 19, then 16, and a prostitute, met up with **Soi Ket Dang**, 32, through MeetMe.com. Dang, a produce manager at a supermarket, paid Randall $140 for sex at their first meeting.

He and Randall then agreed on a price of $350 for a second meeting but he was dissatisfied with her services at the second meeting and offered her $60 or $80 instead. Dang said Randall pushed him, he wrapped his arms around her and they wrestled to the floor. The altercation moved to the kitchen where Dang picked up a knife and stabbed Randall 2 or 3 times. When she began screaming, he grabbed her throat to stop it, then stabbed her two or three more times. Dang then sat by her body, both of them still naked, for about 40 minutes before he bound her hands and feet, wrapped her in sheets and placed her in the closet. He then drove to Castle Island in South Boston and took a nap in his car.

Another woman on MeetMe.com then contacted Dang asking him to meet her. Dang brought her to his home and told her he had killed a woman the night before, that her body was in the house, and not to step in the blood on the floor. The witness reporting seeing blood in Dang's house and the possibility of a body. The teenager's cell phone was tracked to Dang's address in Halifax, Nova Scotia. When Halifax Police arrived at Dang's house, Dang invited them in without any objection. Police observed what they believed to be blood on the floor, which Dang claimed was "leftover blood" from tattoo clients. One of the officers spotted blood-stained sheets in a closet and what looked to be a body wrapped in a blanket. Dang was arrested November 18, 2015 and charged with Murder.

9

(Zoosk.com)

Wendi Davidson and Brian Chevalier

VILLAINOUS VALENTINE

Wendi Davidson, 49, from Massachusetts, met **Brian Chevalier,** 51, on
<u>Zoosk</u> where he posted his profile in early 2004 and they met offline right
away. By Valentine's Day, February 14, 2018, they were engaged.

At some point between February 14 and March, she was having second
thoughts and confided to a friend that Chevalier was "controlling and prone
to angry outbursts."   In late March or early April, she did a deeper search
into his past and discovered his 2004 conviction and 14-year sentence he had
served for a 2003 Kidnapping while on probation for a Burglary. The
Kidnapping charge was for "laying in wait" at the home of a 33-year old ex-
girlfriend. When she got home from work, he tied her to her bed with duct
tape, beat and sexually assaulted her, choked her to the point where she
passed out. The ordeal lasted 21 hours. He said he was going to hide her
body in a freezer when she regained consciousness, so decided to let her live
if she would drive him back to his car and not call police. But on February
19, Davidson's body was found in her basement by a neighbor who alerted
Davidson's brother who called police. Chevalier was arrested in California
where a trial was to be scheduled once is it was known whether Chevalier
will waive extradition back to Massachusetts.

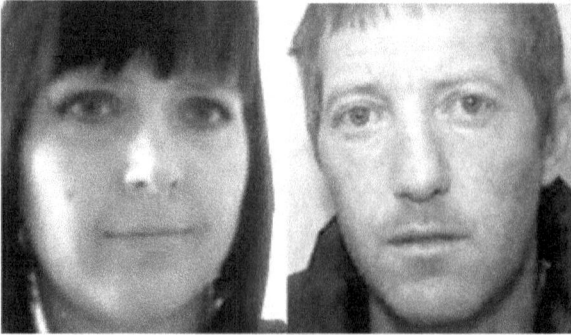

Clare Wood and George Appleton

NOT "RELATIVELY SANE" ENOUGH

In 2008, **Clare Wood**, 36, who had a 10-year old daughter, posted on Zoosk: *"I am a talkative, affectionate woman who would love to hear from someone who is **relatively sane** in my area…a respectful, affectionate man. Not looking for a one-night stand."* In 2008, Wood met **George Appleton,** 40, on Zoosk.

Unemployed and using several aliases, Appleton contacted women via several dating websites, listing his activities as *"Wouldn't ya like to know"* and his interests as *"Music, computers, DJ-ing, films."* Unknown to Wood, who believed his criminal record was only for motoring offenses, Appleton, actually had a history of violence against women, including having been jailed 3 years for harassing a woman in 2002, and, prior to that, he was jailed for 6 years for breaching a restraining order. Wood found that Appleton was obsessive and violent -- enough so, that she repeatedly contacted the Greater Manchester Police (GMP) claiming Appleton had caused criminal damage, harassed, threatened to kill her, and sexually assaulted her. She had a panic alarm installed at her home after making an allegation of Attempted Rape resulting in his arrest for smashing down her front door.

A week later, in February 2009, Wood's father had trouble contacting his daughter and asked his son-in-law to visit her home. That's when Wood's body was found at her home in Salford. She had been strangled and set on fire by Appleton. Women on major dating sites were warned not to meet up with Appleton as police immediately began hunting for him. Six days later, Appleton was found hanged in a dive bar. An inquest into his death found he had committed suicide.

10

FiendFinder

(AdultFriendFinder.com)

*"It's the easiest thing in the world.
Just point, pull the trigger, and people go away."*
-Obie Williams, "The Crimes of Orphans"

Rachel, baby Lillian, and Neil Entwistle

MOST EVIL

On January 20, 2006, **Neil Entwistle,** 29, had joined <u>Adult Friend Finder,</u> which describes itself as "the world's largest sex and swinger personals community, in the week before he shot to death his wife, **Rachel Souza Entwistle**, 27, and their 9-month old daughter, **Lilian Rose Entwistle.**

Neil Entwistle was described by all as a loving, doting husband and father. Rachel Souza, an American, met and married Neil while she was studying at York University in England and where Neil, raised in England, obtained his Masters Degree in electronic engineering. The Entwistles had just moved to the U.S., found that because Neil and Rachel were at the time unemployed, they could not qualify for a mortgage, so they rented a townhome in Hopkinton, Massachusetts for £1350 per month. Although Neil owned a BMW, he appeared to have "plenty of money" and assured his wife he had $10,000 per month income, he was running up $30,000 in credit card debt and his financial pressures were mounting.

On the day of the killings, he told his wife he had a job interview but the interview didn't work out so he went shopping for computer parts. But there had been no job interview. The day after shooting his wife and child, Entwistle drove 50 miles to his in-laws' house and returned a .22 caliber handgun he had taken earlier from his father-in-law's gun case. He then left his car at Boston's Logan International Airport, bought a one-way ticket back to England, and boarded the flight with no luggage. Police found the bodies 2 days later, under a pile of bedding, after being called by concerned relatives who could not reach the couple, searched the home but hadn't noticed the bodies.

Entwistle claimed that on the day of the killings, when he returned from errands, he found his wife and baby dead, and was so distraught that that he contemplated suicide himself with a knife but could not go through with it, so went to his inlaws' house and started to take the gun but panicked and "went into a trance-like state" to explain why he failed to tell police and fled back to Britain on a one-way ticket. After being extradited back to Massachusetts, he blamed his wife, claiming it had to be a murder-suicide because of post-natal depression. But his DNA that was found on the grip of the gun and matched DNA from Rachel that was found on the gun muzzle. Psychologists believe his behavior was due to Asperger Syndrome.

During his 2008 trial, it emerged that Entwistle had begun looking to cheat on his wife even before the couple relocated to the States in the summer of 2005. He had posted on a swingers website looking for a "discreet relationship" and included a graphic nude snapshot of himself. And in the days leading up the murders, he was trawling websites in the Boston area looking for female escorts. Even behind bars, his cravings did not change. And while in jail awaiting trial, in one of a series of creepy sex letters to Heather Standaelt, 4, a mother of two who thought he was innocent, his lie to an investigator about his whereabouts at the time of the murders was exposed in his own words. He revealed to her that he "saw his wife die" and had pondered what went through her and their baby's mind as the child yelled out in pain – "Was she calling for her Daddy to come help?" She then knew he was a murderer. After sending Heather a Bible and writing her about how he had "found God," he told Heather he could no longer contain himself and wanted to seduce her and wanted her assurance, which she provided with a photo, that her legs "look slender but not thin because "I want a leg that looks like it can handle my firm grip in the moment of passion but I don't want it too big… or I could spend a lifetime looking for the perfect leg."

Neil Entwistle was sentenced to Life Without Parole.

> *"Murder isn't the most logical way to escape a difficult situation.
> It only leads to a different situation."*
> -Keigo Higashino, "The Devotion of Suspect X"

Robyn Gardner and Gary Giordano

A VACATION TO DIE FOR

Robyn Gardner, 35, met **Gary Giordano**, 50, on <u>Adult Friend Finder</u>. On August 2, 2011, Gardner supposedly drowned in Aruba while allegedly snorkeling with "traveling companion" Giordano. In the weeks since her disappearance, evidence was built substantially against Giordano, the only suspect in the very dense, high profile, ongoing case.

Giordano was initially held in Aruba, joined by his defense attorney, Jose Baez, who helped Casey Anthony get acquitted of murder earlier in 2011. Speculation grew after it was learned that Gardner had a live-in boyfriend, **Richard Forester**, 40, at her home in Gaithersburg, Maryland, who knew that Gardner and Giordano had argued before they left for Aruba. Gardner had been laid off from her job at a dental practice and was strapped for cash. Dubbed the "American Beauty" by TV personality Nancy Grace, it was debated whether Gardner was paid as a prostitute to travel with Giordano, or was cheating on Forester, or was an innocent victim, or something in between. In any case, things didn't add up. Although it appeared that this was certainly a murder, all anyone could do was hope that it was just a matter of time before Giordano would be suffocated by his mountain of lies.

A former girlfriend of Giordano's who obtained a restraining order after Giordano stalked her, secretly videotaped them having sex and posted pornographic images of Gardner on Internet. Another woman who had dated Giordano, Jeanette Farago, told The Washington Post that Giordano had stalked and harassed her, shoring up outside her window wearing a deer face mask illuminating his face the dark with his cigarette lighter – which she called "really creepy and scary" and at one point offering to take her on a 2-week cruise but when he sent her aggressively harmful texts, she backed out of the cruise. At the time of Gardner's disappearance, Giordano was in serious financial trouble and attempted to scam a staffing company out of $5-million with fabricated documents. He also had a history of theft, from individual for up to $500 and for shoplifting jewelry at Costco. Within 2 days after reporting Gardner missing, Giordano attempted to redeem an accidental death insurance policy on Gardner that could be worth $1.5-million, which raised an alarm as it was an excessive amount for a week long trip and Gardner's boyfriend, Forester, said he knew nothing about the insurance policy which she would never have signed voluntarily.

A witness alleged he saw Giordano grab Gardner by her neck and threatened to kill her as he shoved her into an elevator on the last day she was seen alive. Police found Ambien, a sleep medication, prescribed to Gardner in the Marriott Hotel room where she was staying with Giordano and Giordano told police he saw her take a sleeping pill the day he claims they went snorkeling and she never returned. A friend and family member told police Gardner was a "sneaky drinker" and witnesses who saw Gardner the day she vanishes described her as drunk and woozy. Giordano was initially arrested at the airport trying to make his way back to the U.S., 3 days after reporting Gardner missing. When asked about his "travel companion," Giordano reportedly responded "She's taking another flight." And investigators had a difficult time identifying Giordano on surveillance videos due to the number of times he changed his toupees. Authorities said they found blood on a rock behind the dive shop at Run Reef where the two were last seen together after allegedly snorkeling but drove away without ever going in the water. It then appeared that Giordano was trying to be seen on every surveillance camera to establish an alibi. Meanwhile police received a tip from a man who claimed Giordano put a bag over Gardner's head, tied up her limbs with duct tape, drove her to Dog Graves Beach where dogs were known to be buried, dug up a fresh dog's grave with his bare hands, widened the hole, put Robyn into the grave, put the dead dog's body on top of hers and then she started moaning and moving while he filled up the hole. Cadaver dogs were used to search for Gardner's remains but Gardner was never found.

In 2014, Giordano wrote a book, "*The Aruba Files (The Redemption of Gary V. Giordano)*" in an effort to exculpate himself from the matter. But on April 7, 2017, Gary Giordano was found liable for the Wrongful Death of Robyn Gardner in a civil trial, because the Plaintiff, Robyn's sister, was able to prove that he was responsible "by a preponderance of evidence."

Jay Stone and Thomas Heath

FEARSOME THREESOME

Jay Stone, 30, met **Thomas "Mike" Heath,** 35, and his wife, **Shanna Heath,** on <u>Adult Friend Finder</u>, a website geared to people who are married and want to meet up with others for sex. Stone, a Disney-Orlando custodian with learning disabilities, the son of a top official in the Orange County Public Defender's office, was socially awkward but with sexual desires like anyone else and so met the couple for sex at a Kissimmee, Florida motel. Their emails that followed their encounter said they had a good time with each other. Later, the Heaths told Stone that they and their two toddlers were about to get kicked out of their motel room because they could not come up with the rent. Stone, described by many as a kind, generous person, offered to let the family stay with him, and on August 14, 2012, the Heath family moved into Stone's one-bedroom apartment and Stone got them Disney tickets and bought them food.

Nine days later, August 23, 2012, a fight broke out at Stone's apartment and Heath strangled Stone to death with a power cord. Stone's body was found in his closet, covered in clothing with his hands bound by a belt. Heath claimed he killed Stone to prevent him from raping his wife, Shanna, with whom Stone already had consensual sex, when Stone began demanding sex with Shanna in exchange for letting them move in. After murdering Stone, the Heaths stole his electronics and his car. Shanna Heath was in the Orange County Jail for lying about the murder under oath. Mike Heath was convicted of First Degree Murder in the death of Jay Stone as well as Robbery With a Deadly Weapon and Carjacking and given 3 Life sentences.

11
bumble
killer bees

(bumble.com)

Laureline Garcia-Bertaux

CASE PENDING

The body of **Laureline Garcia-Bertaux**, 34, a French National from Corsica who had been living in London for 10 years, was found in a shallow grave in her garden. Detectives probing her love life after friends said she was active on dating apps including <u>Bumble</u>, were trying to trace a man who she was going to meet for coffee Sunday evening after being last seen alive with a man on CCTV, shopping for groceries at a supermarket, and was reported missing by co-workers on Monday when failed to show up for work. Friends say timing of Laureline's <u>Bumble</u> date was "a bit suspicious."

And yet, her Russian ex-boyfriend, Kiril Belorusov, 32, a tall, shaven headed barman from Estonia, the only confirmed suspect, who had been celebrating his birthday Friday night, was charged with her Murder, pled Not Guilty, and is awaiting trial scheduled for September 9, 2019.

Laureline lived alone after splitting with Belorusov in 2018. Her Rottweiler and Husky dogs were still in her rented ground floor flat in Kew, West London, and she had planned to move out of that house Monday morning. Laureline, described as "amazing," dreamed of becoming a film-maker, worked at the Discovery Channel; and ran a creative video production firm called Black Balloons Studio, worked with Goli, a PR firm, and had worked with Dame Joan Collins on the movie, "Gerry."

Rudolph Smith,   Whitney Herd,   George Zimmerman,   David Gabrielli

BUMBLE'S FUMBLES

Rudolph Jericho Smith, 34, of Frederick, Maryland, was arrested on April 15, 2019 and indicted by a Frederick County grand jury on 4 counts of First Degree Assault, Reckless Endangerment and Knowing Transferring HIV to Another Person, following a 22-month investigation indicating he knowingly spread the deadly HIV virus to numerous women he met on Bumble dating website since July 2017

Whitney Wolfe Herd, Bumble founder, created the dating website to make it "acceptable for women to make the first move." Herd, herself, had reportedly been receiving death threats, not from Smith's victims but from *gun owners* who didn't like Herd's decision to ban images of guns from Bumble's site in the wake of school shootings and other mass shootings.

George Zimmerman, 35, who made headlines in 2012 when he shot and killed unarmed Trayvon Martin, 17, while Zimmerman was working as a neighborhood watch volunteer, and who was acquitted in his 2013 trial and who in 2018 pleaded No Contest to **Stalking** a private investigator, was kicked off Bumble *twice*, and also from Tinder, for creating a phony profile with a fake name, "Carter."

David Gabrielli, 37, a divorced French father of two, is accused of raping a woman, 26, January 30, 2018, on a first date, who he met on Bumble by posing as a doctor, with screen name "Doctor Dave," when he connected with the victim in Maroubra, East Sydney, Australia. After his arrest, two more women, ages 40 and 26, came forward with similar claims and additional charges were filed. Gabrielli was arrested after a 7-month investigation charged with 2 counts of Indecent Assault, 2 counts of Aggravated Sexual Assault Without Consent, and Hindering a Person Executing a Crime Scene."

12

badoo

bad boys

(badoo.com)

Mary Tiburcio, Sierra Seucallius, Arian Lozano, Ashita Bista;   Nicholas Mextasas
Livia Bunea, Elena Bunea, Maricar Arquilola

THE BADOO SERIAL KILLER

Mary Rose Tiburcio, 38, and her daughter, **Sierra Graze Seucallius**, 6, from the Philippines, were reported missing by Tiburcio's roommate on May 5, 2018, when Tiburcio and her daughter never returned from a date. Detectives learned she had gone to meet someone names "Orestis" who she connected with on the dating app, Badoo. Nearly a year later, in April 2019, a tourist snapping photos at an abandoned copper mine on the island of Cyprus spotted Tiburcio's body that recent storms caused to float to the top of a flooded mine shaft.   Authorities used remote cameras to search for Tiburcio's 6-year old daughter, Sierra, without success.

A few days later, on April 20, in the same Cyprus mine shaft where Tiburcio had been discovered, police found another victim, **Arian Palanas Lozano**, 28, who was also Filippino and who had been missing since July 21, 2018. Tiburcio, and her young daughter, and Lozano were the tip of the iceberg of violence against migrant women in Cyprus

Within days of finding Tiburcio and Lozano, police were on the trail of **Nicholas Mextasas**, 35, a Greek Cypriot National Guard captain and father of two, who at first refused to cooperate with police but eventually signed a 10-page confession 7 killings of foreign women who had come to his tourist-driven Mediterranean island for work.   Upon capture, Mextases, the first serial killer on Cyprus, spent weeks guiding police to the places where he dumped other victims.   He told police that after killing 6-year old Sierra, he dumped her body in Xylatou Lake but divers never found the child.

When Mextasas led police to another victim, **Maricar Valdez, Arquiola**, 31, from the Philippines; who had been missing since December 13, 2017 and whose body was recovered from a well on an Army firing range, and who had been missing since December 13, 2017, he was initially charged with 4 murders before police recovered bodies of 2 more women from an abandoned mine shaft in Mitsero.

The other victims of Nicholas Mextasas were: **Livia Florentina Bunea**, 36, a Romanian woman, and her daughter, **Elena Natalia Bunea**, 8, both of whom were missing since September 30, 2016; and **Ashita Khadka Bista**, from Nepal, who had never been reported missing.

Mary Rose Tiburcio's 6-year old daughter, Sierra, remains missing.

Mextasas pleaded guilty to Premeditated Murder and Kidnapping of the first 4 women and girls. He apologized to the families of his victims for the "unjust pain" he had caused. A 3-judge panel said he deliberately targeted the most "defenseless" of victims and that he "didn't even hesitate to kill children" during the 2-1/2 years that he sought out his adult victims through online dating networks.

Mextasas was give a Life sentence via 7 sentences of 25 years each for a total of 175 years.

Tim Smith   Mark Law and Mason Casey

MURDEROUS MEETUP

Tim Smith, 45, a fork lift instructor, was stabbed in the heart while in his car, after meeting up with **Mark Anthony Law**, 20, and **Mason Casey,** 18, in Shepshed, Leicestershire, England. Law had sent Smith an indecent image of himself via the dating-focused social networking app, Badoo, and then suggested they meet for a threesome.

On March 16, 2017, the night of the murder, Smith, from Staffordshire, had arranged to pick up Law from his home. Casey then joined them in the car and Smith drove to Gelders Hall Industrial Estate where they parked. Casey claimed he had no idea that Law was carrying a knife, that he was going to murder Smith, nor that there had been a suggestion of group sex. Law suddenly stabbed Smith and the two men ran off. Smith was able to put the car into reverse in an attempt to drive away but collided with a wall at the entrance and collapsed. Smith died at the scene.

The court heard that Law had harbored fantasies about cannibalism, chopping people up and sadism. In a plea bargain, Law pleaded guilty to Murder, while Casey was found guilty by a jury, and both were sentenced to Life in prison.

13

craigslist®
carnage

Katherine Olson and Michael Anderson

THE FIRST EVER "CRAIGSLIST KILLER"

Michael John Anderson, 19, a resident of Savage, Minnesota posted 14 ads on Craigslist in the fall of 2007, posing variously as a photographer, a producer, and also mother named "Amy" looking for a baby sitter. He was trolling for models, for women with sexy voices, and for sitter who wanted a job as a nanny or babysitter. After an exchange of emails and cell phone calls, with college student **Katherine Ann Olson,** 24, he lured to his home, alleging needing a babysitter for a 5-year old girl, "just so he could experience what it felt like to kill someone." On October 25, 2007, Anderson shot Olson with a .357 magnum, put her body in the trunk of her car, then drove to Burnsville Nature Preserve where she was discovered the next day. Media labeled him *"The Craigslist Killer."*

Psychiatrists for the Defense diagnosed Anderson with Aspergers Syndrome, a form of Autism, contending the developmental disability made him unable to foresee potential outcomes, while the Prosecution showed the murder was premeditated. The judge refused to allow evidence of the Aspergers diagnosis to be presented in court, ruling there was no proof that the disorder was connected to the crime and that it could invite jurors to speculate about "diminished capacity" which is "not recognized in Minnesota." The Prosecutor said Anderson bragged *"I'm Famous – I'm The Craigslist Murderer."* Anderson was found guilty if First Degree Murder and received a sentence of Life Without Parole. On Appeal, the Supreme Court of Minnesota affirmed the verdict in 2014.

Richard Beasley, Brogan Rafferty   Timothy Kern, Ralph Geiger, David Pauley

THE $5 KILLER

Richard "Jack" Beasley and his accomplice, **Brogan Rafferty,** then-16, placed ads on Craigslist offering farmhand jobs in order to lure men to a cattle ranch outside Akron, Ohio in 2011, he didn't want his victims to be completely down and out. He needed men on the margins, yes, but not so marginal that they didn't have some possessions worth killing for – a truck or a TV or a computer or even a motorcycle. Police say it was Beasley who shot and killed their victims — **Timothy Kern**, 47, **Ralph Geiger, 56,** and **David Pauley, 51**— and wounded Scott Davis, 49, who was shot in the arm and survived.

Rafferty later told the investigators, "because as the story goes on and on, I'm realizing that I'm about to help Beasley do this for no reason at all. Not that I even wanted to do it at all. But it takes, like, all the minimal sanity and reason out of doing this … It would be like if a lion killed a zebra just to kill it … Just 'cause it wanted, like, its hoof or something. The man literally had just $5 in his pocket."

The jury recommended Execution after hearing 2 hours of testimony from witnesses, including Beasley's tearful mother, Carol Beasley, who testified that her son had a troubled childhood and suffered physically abuse by his stepfather and sexual abuse by neighborhood youngsters, stating "I always felt there was more than he told me. Beasley was convicted of 3 counts of Aggravated Murder and one count of Attempted Murder and is currently on Ohio's Death Row.

Rafferty, who was a juvenile at the time of the crimes, is currently serving a Life sentence.

Miranda Barbour, Elyette Barbour, Tony LaFerrara

THE NEWLYWED KILLERS

Miranda Barbour, 19, and her husband, **Elyette Barbour,** 22, "wanted to kill someone together." So they lured a stranger, **Tony LeFerrara**, 42, an electrical engineer, with a <u>Craigslist</u> ad promising "companionship" in exchange for $100. When Laferrara got in their car, her husband of 3 weeks was hiding under a blanket in the back seat. Miranda first gave LaFerrara an "out" by telling him she was actually 16. When he indicated he still wanted to have sex with her, Miranda was to say the code words, *"Did you see the stars tonight?"* and Elyette was then supposed to leap from the back seat with a cord, wrap it around LaFerrara's throat and choked him to death. But when Elyette missed his cue and LaFerrara slid his hand higher up on her thigh, Miranda pulled a knife from the side pocket of her car door and plunged it into LaFerrara's chest, again and again – 20 times. They dumped his body in an alley. After scrubbing their blood soaked passenger seat, they celebrated at a strip club.

Miranda Barbour says *"If he had done the right thing, he would still be alive."* She claims she killed between 22 and 45 other people, starting at age 13, in at least 4 other states and that she has no regrets about LaFrerra, stating *'I didn't hurt anyone who didn't deserve it."*

119

Phillip Markoff and Julissa Brisman

HE RUBBED HER THE WRONG WAY

Phillip Haynes Markoff, 22, met victim **Julissa Brisman**, 26, via his
<u>Craigslist</u> ad for sensual massage in Boston, Massachusetts in 2009. Markoff
allegedly shot Brisman to death on the 20th floor of the Mariott Copley Place
Hotel.

He was suspected of killing 4 other women on a stretch of Gilgo Beach on
Fire Island over at least an 18-month span. While waiting for his trial on
Murder and Armed Robbery charges, Markoff, then 24, committed suicide
in jail.

George Weber and John Katheis

BREAKING NEWS: YOU'RE DEAD

John Katehis, 16, met ABC Radio reporter **George Weber**, 47, a Satanic sado-masochist who agreed to a drug fueled rough sex romp for $60 through Katheis' personal ad on Craigslist in New York City in 2009. Katehis stabbed Weber 50 times in his apartment and claimed self defense during a bad S&M encounter but was convicted of Second Degree Murder at his second trial and sentenced to Life With Possibility of Parole in 2034.

John Burgess and Donna Jou

SHE OVERSTAYED HER WELCOME

John Steven Burgess, 39, met his victim, **Donna Jou,** 19, through Craigslist in Los Angeles, California in 2007. Burgess claims that he supplied Jou with a mixture of heroin and cocaine, known as a "speedball," and alcohol, and that he woke up to find her dead from the accidental overdose in his home before panicking and dumping her body in the ocean, which has not been found. Burgess pleaded guilty to Involuntary Manslaughter and was sentenced to 5 Years in Prison. He was paroled after 2 years in July 2014. He had failed to register as a Sex Offender after a previous conviction for Lewd and Lascivious Conduct with a Minor and is now registered.

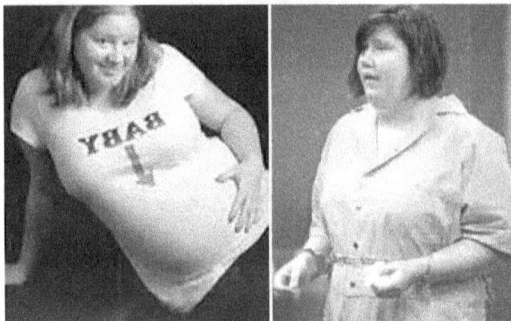

Heather Snively and Korena Roberts

MOTHERHOOD BY MURDER

Korena Roberts met her victim, **Heather Snively**, 21, in 2009 on Craigslist where she purported to sell baby clothes to the pregnant woman. Snively met Roberts in Washington County, Oregon, at her home where Roberts hit the pregnant woman up to 30 times, cut open her abdomen, having planned a Fetal Abduction. Snively died of major blood loss; the baby was also pronounced dead. Roberts pleaded guilty October 6, 2010 to Aggravated Murder and was sentenced to Life in Prison Without Possibility of Parole.

Haroon Khan   Tammi LaFave, Travis Zoellick

CARJACK CASUALTY

Tammi LaFave, 21, and **Travis Zoellick,** 20, met their victim, **Haroon Khan,** 31, through his Craigslist ad for his car in 2009 in Milwaukee, Wisconsin. During the test drive, Zoellick stabbed him to death; they then hid his car in a garage. Lafave claimed Travis did the killing and she just went along with it "so he wouldn't break up with her."

Zoellick killed himself prior to arrest. LaFave pleaded guilty to felony Murder and is serving a 25-year sentence.

Youa Lor and Dao Xiong

FROM HOT CAR PARTS TO MAKING LICENSE PLATES

Dao Xiong, 19, responded to a <u>Craigslist</u> ad posted by his victim, **Youa "Ty" Lor,** 33, who was selling his car in Lake Elmo, Minnesota in 2010, intending to steal the vehicle and sell it for parts. While on the test drive, Xiong shot Lor, threw him out of the car and drove away. Xiong was convicted of 3 counts of Murder and is serving a Life Without Possibility of Parole.

NOT SO EASY RIDER

Brandon Kent, 26, met his victim, **Thai Lam,** 26, to look at a motorcycle Lam was advertising for sale on <u>Craigslist</u> in Savannah, Georgia in 2010. Kent shot Lam in his garage before fleeing the scene on Lam's motorcycle. Police apprehended Kent nearly an hour later. Kent pleaded guilty to Murder and is serving a Life sentence.

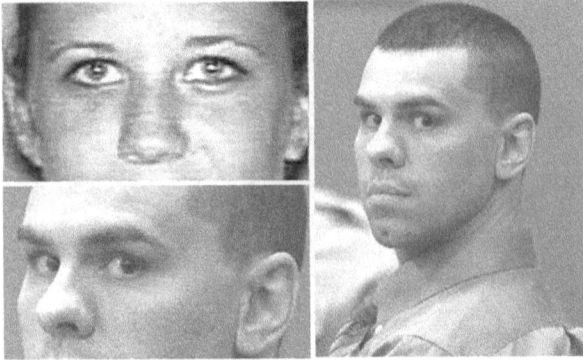

Amy Dickey and Nathaniel Briscoe

MORE THAN SHE BARGAINED FOR

Nathaniel Briscoe, 30, met his victim, **Amy Elizabeth Dickey**, 28, who placed ads for sex on Craigslist, in Austin, Texas in 2010. When Dickey met Briscoe at his apartment, he strangled her to death, then dumped her body in a field. During his trial he admitted to putting his hands around her throat during sex, but claimed she left his apartment that night. Briscoe was convicted of Murder and is serving a sentence of Life With the Possibility of Parole as early as 2039.

Chad Johnson and Jennifer Papain

DISSATISFIED CUSTOMER

Chad Johnson, 23, met his victim, **Jennifer Papain**, 26, through a prostitution ad on Craigslist in Medford, New York in 2010. Johnson strangled Papain *after she refused to give him an $80 refund*, and buried her body in a shallow grave near his home. Johnson was convicted of Second Degree Murder and is serving a sentence of Life With Possibility of Parole as early as 2035.

Diane Warrick

CRAZY CAREGIVER

Diane Cheryl Warrick, 56, met her victim, **Mary Jane Scanlon**, 70, when she responded to Scanlon's Craigslist ad for a caretaker in Pleasant Hill, California in 2010. Warrick stabbed Scanlon to death in her bed and claimed that she was hallucinating at the time. Warrick had a violent history of robbery and hostage-taking in Colorado and California. Warrick was convicted of Murder and is serving a sentence of 31 Years to Life.

Phillip Boldon and Sarah Weyrick

BLOOD MONEY

Phillip Erric Boldon, 31, met his victim, **Sarah Weyrick**, 19, who posted a Personals ad in the "Casual Encounters" section on Craigslist in Houston, Texas in 2010, saying she was having trouble paying her bills and desperate times call for desperate measures. He murdered her the day they met, May 31 or June 1, and on June 2 she was found stabbed to death in her burning car. Boldon was soon arrested for her murder. The cash he paid his drug dealer, Howard Martin, had Weyrick's blood on it. Boldon was convicted of Murder and is serving Life With Possibility of Parole early as 2040.

BETTER THAN SEX

David Kelsey Sparre, 19, met his victim, **Tiara Poole**, 21, who was "looking for a friend" via a <u>Craigslist</u> personal ad in Jacksonville, Florida in 2011. When Sparre met Poole, they drove to her home where he stabbed her to death 89 times and fled in her car. Sparre first claimed he flew into a rage after they had sex and she told him she was married with children but divorcing; he also said he had previously killed someone with a gun but figured getting close up while stabbing Poole would be a "good rush" and "I enjoyed it and hoped to do it again." Sparre was convicted of First Degree Murder and is on Florida's Death Row.

Alexander Lyons and Lamar Clemons

THE $95 MURDER

Alexander D. Lyons, 23, and his accomplice, **Lamar DeAngelo Clemons**, 19, met up with their victim, **Johnathan Clements**, 19, on the pretense of selling him a phone, in response to Clements' Craigslist want-ad seeking to buy an Android cell phone, in Detroit, Michigan in 2011. The plan was to rob Clement of the $95 cash he was to pay for the phone but Lyons shot and killed Clements. Lyons and Clemons are serving Life sentences for Murder.

JUST FRIENDS

Latoya Jordan, 24, met **Daniel S. Somerson**, 53, a former trucker in Fountain, Florida, in 2011 through <u>Craigslist</u> where she routinely looked to find a man to live with. Jordan admitted to police that she stabbed Somerson 30 times, 4 days after moving in with him, because "he was looking for love and she wasn't interested – He was going to kick her out, and she did not want to be homeless." Jordan was found guilty of First Degree Murder and sentenced to Life in Prison Without Possibility of Parole.

Thomas Bashline and Draton Mares

DEADLY WORDS

Draton Mares, 23, met his victim, **Thomas Bashline,** 42, a trainer for the Harlem Globetrotters, via a personal ad on <u>Craigslist</u> in Denver, Colorado in 2011. The pair met several times for sex, until Mares shot Bashline in the back of the head, murdering him before fleeing in Bashline's car. Mares was triggered to shoot because Bashline became aggressive, called Mares a "fag" and other derogatory remarks. Mares was convicted of First Degree Murder, and is serving Life Without Possibility of Parole.

Garrett Berki   Shaquille Jordan, Rashon Abernathy, Seandell Jones

CHASING DEATH

Rashon Abernathy, 17, **Shaquille Jordan,** 17, and **Seandell Jones**, 17, met their victims, **Garrett Berki**, 18, and his girlfriend, in San Diego, under the pretense of selling an old a laptop computer for $600 from a Craigslist ad in 2011. The three teens robbed Berki and his girlfriend of $600 and their phones and fled. Berki drove after the trio to get their license plate number and was shot and killed Berki during the pursuit. Abernathy was convicted of Murder and got 50-Years. Jordan and Jones each got 25 Years to Life.

James Sanders - Clabon Berniard, Amanda Knight, Kiyoshi Higashi, Joshua Reese

DIAMONDS ARE FOREVER – AND A CAUSE OF DEATH

Kiyoshi Higashi, 22, and his accomplices, **Joshua N. Reese,** 20, **Amanda Christine Knight**, 21, and **Clabon Berniard**, 23, met their victim, **James Sanders, Sr**, 43, who ran a Craigslist ad for a diamond ring, in Edgewood, Washington in April 2010. In a violent home invasion, Sanders was shot to death in front of his wife Charlene and their sons Jim Jr, 14, and Chandler, 11. Berniard was convicted of Murder and got a 124 Year sentence. Higashi was convicted of First Degree Murder, First Degree Burglary, Second Degree Assault and is serving a 109-year sentence. Jordan and Jones were both convicted of Murder and each got a 100-year sentence.

Kurt Milliman   Timothy Smith, Kimberly Smith

SHE JUST SAID NO

Timothy S. Smith, 26, and his wife **Kimberly A. Smith,** 28, met the victim, **Kurt Milliman**, 48, who responded to Smith's Personals as on <u>Craigslist</u> offering sex with his pregnant wife but when Kimberly refused to have sex with Milliman, an argument ensured and Timothy, who had been secretly watching, shot and killed Merriman from behind. Timothy Smith was convicted of Murder and sentenced to 50 Years in Prison.

Yuri Ives and Ali Cubba

OVERKILL

Ali Cubba, 17, met the victim, **Yuri Ansel Ives**, 54, through <u>Craigslist</u> in Kansas City, Missouri in 2011. Court records do not indicate the nature of the connection. Cubba admitted he met Ives at his home with the intention of robbing him, stabbed him 23 times and shot him twice in the head, killing him. The judge reduced Cubba's plea deal to 15 Years for Second Degree Murder and 10 years for Armed Criminal Action, concurrent.

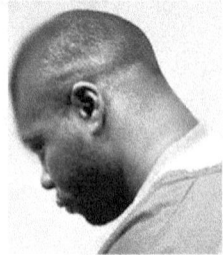

Josimar Rojas, Irene Reyes, Susana Rueles   Jade Harris

CHEVY CHASE

In 2012, **Jade Douglas Harris,** 30, responded to a <u>Craigslist</u> ad selling a 2010 Chevy Camaro in downtown Downy, California, intending to steal the car. When Harris realized the car wasn't on the premises, he shot and killed **Josimar Rojas,** 26, and **Irene Cardenas Reyes,** 35, then forced **Susan Perez Ruelas,** 34, to drive him to the family's home to see the car, and shot her to death in front of her son, 13, who Harris also shot, although the boy survived. Harris was found with the car and was charged with 3 counts of Murder, 3 counts of Kidnapping for Carjacking, 3 counts of Carjacking, 2 counts of Attempted Murder, 2 counts of Kidnapping, and 1 count of Possession of a Firearm by a Felon.

William Aps   Isaac Williams, Jquan Scott

CHEVY PICKUP PLAN BACKFIRED

Jquan Margel Scott, 19, and **Isaac Romell Williams**, 20, met victim **Isaac Williams**. Scott met up with victim **William Alexander "Alex" Apps,** 25, at a Hardees restaurant in Charleston, South Carolina, in 2013 in response to Apps' <u>Craigslist</u> offering his Chevy pickup truck for sale. Apps was shot in the neck and left in the woods. Williams and Scott, last people to have seen Apps, were tracked by the victim's phone and bank records. Williams was convicted of Murder and sentenced to Life Without Parole. Scott, got 40 Years in Prison for Murder and Armed Robbery.

Larry Wilkins   Brandon Vance, Martiness Henderson, Walter Collins

MUSTANG MURDER #1

On May 9, 2014, **Larry Wilkins,** 37, a FedEx package handler, advertised his restored 2006 Ford Mustang for sale on Craigslist. Wilkins worked nights, so **Brandon Vance**, 17, agreed to meet him close to midnight in the parking lot at Wilkins' apartment complex. Vance, accompanied by **Martiness Henderson**, 17, and **Walter Collins**, 17, intended to just steal the car, but when they realized it had a manual transmission and Collins was the only one who could drive a stick shift, Vance was annoyed and fatally shot Wilkins while the car was still moving. They dumped Wilkins body in his parking lot and fled. Vance was charged with First Degree Murder While Committing a Robbery.

June and Elrey Runion - and Ronnie Towns

MUSTANG MURDER #2

Elrey "Bud" Runion, 69, and his wife, **June Runion,** 66, drove 3-1/2 hours from Atlanta, Georgia to see a classic 1966 Mustang advertised on Craigslist. Their car was recovered from a pond near their bodies in the woods in rural Telfair County. **Ronnie "Jay" Adrian Towns,** 28, who fatally shot the couple in their heads, was charged with Murder and Armed Robbery.

131

Kent Storrer   Jacob Marshall, Jerry Kimball

MITSUBISHI MURDER

Kent Wayne Storrer, 53, was helping his son-in-law, **Jasper Qualls**, 32, sell his 1991 Mitsubishi 3000 VR4 via a Craigslist ad. **Jacob Lyn Marshall**, 20, accompanied by **Jerry Burton Kimball**, 22, took the car for a test drive intending to steal the car. Using an AR-15 assault rifle, Marshall shot both Storrer and Qualls. Qualls was treated for his wound and released from the hospital but Storrer died. Marshall pled guilty to First Degree Murder and two other felonies to avoid the Death Penalty, and got 70 Years in Prison; Kimball, charged Murder and 5 other felonies, got 45 Years in Prison.

Avery Cornuelle and Peyton McAnelly

YOUR MONEY OR YOUR LIFE (OR BOTH)

Avery Cornuelle, 21, and accomplice **Peyton McAnelly,** 23, met their victim, **Joseph Givens,** 45, through an alternative lifestyle ad on Craigslist in O'Fallon, Missouri in 2012, intending to rob Givens but their attempted robbery went wrong and Corneulle and McAnelly stabbed Givens to death. Cornuelle was convicted of Second Degree Murder and is serving a 25-year sentence. McAnelly was charged with Second Degree Murder, Armed Criminal Action, and Attempted Robbery.

James Vester   Tyshaune Kincade, Tryon Kincade

ICED I-PAD BUYER'S LAST BREATH IDs KILLER

Tyshaune Kincade, 18, and his brother **Tryon Kincade,** 19, lured victim, **James Vester,** 32, with a <u>Craigslist</u> ad for an iPad that Vester was wanting to buy for his mother. They shot and killed Vester, in Indianapolis, Indiana in December 2013. Before he died at the hospital, that the suspects took keys to his vehicle, his cell phone, his wallet, $250 cash and he gave cops the phone numbers they used to call him. Tyshaune got 50 Years in Prison for and Robbery. Tryon got 35 Years in Prison. parking lot of an Oak Forest restaurant and fled into a nearby forest preserve.

Aung Bo and Steve Lewis

ICED I-PHONE BUYER'S CLUMSY KILLER

In 2012, **Steven Emmanuel Lewis,** 27, offered an I-Phone for sale in his Craigslist ad. **Aung Thu Bo,** 19, and his girlfriend met Lewis at a restaurant hoping to buy the phone. But Lewis claimed he had left the phone at home and that they should come with him to get it. When the three got in the car, Lewis pulled a gun on the couple demanding their money. Lewis claims the gun went off accidentally, killing Bo and wounding himself in the forearm. He was convicted of Second Degree Murder and Aggravated Robbery and got 24 Years in Prison

Nishant Patel   Dominique Clanton, Bryant Dowdy

NO HONOR AMONG PHONE THIEVES

Dominique Clanton, 18, **Bryant "BeDo" Dowdy,** 21, and **Eric Clanton** met victim **Nishant Patel,** 31, in Indianapolis, Indiana in 2013 through a Craigslist ad in which Patel advertised a phone for sale, intending to rob Patel who the trio robbed and shot to death. Dowdy also shot and killed Eric Clanton, and shot and wounded Dominique Clanton (who survived) in an effort to eliminate witnesses. Dowdy was convicted of Murder of Patel while serving a 75-Year sentence for shooting the Clantons. Dominique Clanton pleaded guilty to Conspiracy to Commit Armed Robbery.

Deanna Ballman and Ali Salim

DOCTOR DEATH

Dr. Ali Salim met **Deanna Ballman**, 23, of Akron, Ohio, a mother of two who was 9 months pregnant, via a Craigslist ad offering sex for $200, in July 2012. Salim gave Ballman, who was not a drug user, a lethal dose of heroin as he wanted to have sex with her while she was incapacitated. Ballman's body was found in her car in the woods. Salim was convicted of 2 counts of Involuntary Manslaughter, Rape, Tampering with Evidence, Abuse of a Corpse, and was sentenced to 36 Years in Prison.

Thomas Mastro and Christopher

MURDER, NO KID'S GAME

The victim, **Thomas Mastro**, 24, met **Christopher Dyson**, 18, via Craigslist, to trade his iPhone for Mastro's PlayStation gaming system outside of a 7-Eleven store in Tinley Park, Michigan, but an argument ensued. The store's outdoor surveillance video shows Dyson placing the boxed PlayStation inside a Mercedes but Mastro retrieved PlayStation and the two began to struggle over it. Dyson pulled out a gun and shot Mastro in the chest, put the PlayStation in his car and sped out of the parking lot. A witness flagged down an off-duty police officer nearby who chased Dyson, at faster than 90 mph before Dyson abandoned his car, ran, and was caught.

Timothy Radford - Christopher Johnson, Christina Guffey

SEX FOR RENT NEVER PAYS

Christopher Jordan Johnson, 23, **and Christina Marie Guffey**, 27 met victim **Timothy Keith Radford,** 54, through Guffey's Craigslist ad in 2013 when Guffey agreed to have sex with Radford in exchange for allowing the homeless couple stay at his Radford's Asheville, North Carolina home. But upon arrival, Guffey changed her mind about having sex and an argument ensued. Johnson shot Radford to death and the couple then robbed the home. Johnson pleaded guilty to Second Degree Murder and Robbery With A Dangerous Weapon, as well as Failing to Register as a Sex Offender in an unrelated case. Guffey was sentenced to 128 to 168 months in state prison.

Jevon Freeman

Terrance Dent, Latrel Irving

A LOSING PROPOSITION

Terrance Justin Dent, 18, met **Jevon Nathan Freeman**, 25, in reply to Freeman's Craigslist ad selling an iPhone, in Lithonia, Georgia in 2013. Dent, who was charged with Murder, Aggravated Assault and Possession of a Weapon, Tampering with Evidence and Furnishing a Pistol to a Minor, admitted he shot Freeman to death and fleeing in a panic, leaving his $240 cash strewn in the ground, then giving the gun to is friend, **Latrel Irving**, 17, who was then charged with Possession of a Weapon by a Minor.

Alize Smith, Jarron Moreland   - Crystal Bottler, Kevin Bottler, Johnny Barker, Brett Boetler

CRAIGLIST LYNCHING

Alize Ramon Smith, 21, and **Jarron Keonte Moreland**, 21, responded to a gun sale ad on Craigslist. They were shot when they got into the back seat of the van occupied by **Kevin Garcia-Bottler**, 22, and his brother, **Brett Bottler**, 16, who phoned their mother, **Crystal Boettler,** 40, whose boyfriend, **Johnny Shane Barker**, 43, helped them remove the bodies, cover them with tarps, attach cinder blocks with chains, at some dismembered them and dumped into a pond. Because all 4 suspects were White, and the victims were Black, social media called the murders "lynchings." Brett Bottler pled guilty to First and Second Degree Murder, Unlawful Removal of a Dead Body, Desecration of a Corpse and Felony Firearm Possession; Kevin Garcia-Bottler, pled guilty as an Accessory; in a plea deal, Kevin Garcia-Bottler was sentenced to 25 years, 15 as probation; Brett Bottler got 30 years. As of May, 2019, Crystal Boettler's and Kevin Barker's cases were still pending.

Jacob Brantner and Fazon Swinton

GUNS REALLY DO KILL PEOPLE

Jacob "Jake" Brantner, 39, was fatally shot in Kansas City on April 3, 2016, when **Fazon K. Swinton**, 19, met Brantner to buy a handgun that Brantner advertised on <u>Craigslist.</u> Swinton grabbed the gun without paying and the two men then wrestled over the gun; they shot each other. Brantner died while Swinton, though injured, fled.

Swinton was convicted of Second Degree Murder, Armed Criminal Action, Attempted Robbery, and Leaving the Scene. He was sentenced to a total of 32 Years in Prison.

Luis Oliva and Billy Delacey

ANOTHER DISSATISFIED CUSTOMER

Billy Joe Delacey, 36, met his victim, **Luis Alberto Vasquez Oliva**, 26, through personal ads the victim posted to <u>Craigslist</u> for male massages in Mesa County, Colorado in 2012. Oliva, a male escort, was found dead in his apartment with multiple head wounds from a hard object. Alleged to have committed a hate crime, Delacey pleaded guilty to Manslaughter in order to avoid a possible Life sentence.

Brooke Slocum, Charles Oppenneer   Brady Oestrike

TOO DESPERATE AND TOO LATE

In July 2014 in Grand Rapids, Michigan, **Brooke Slocum**, age 18 and 8 months pregnant, and her boyfriend, **Charles ("Charlie") Oppenneer,** 25, were desperate for money when she allowed him to sell herself in a sex-for-cash ad on Craigslist. Responding to the ad, **Brady Oestrike**, 31, a loner who worked as a supervisor at a gas company and who was from a well-off family, agreed to pay $120 if Brooke would have sex with him in a public park at night, *with Oppenneer to be present at the meeting*. That was the last time Slocum and Oppenneer were seen alive. Soon after, police discovered Oppenneer's decapitated body under a tree branch and his skull was found on a private property; it evidenced head trauma. But where was Slocum?

For 5 days, while Oestrike's home was under surveillance and police awaited a search warrant, pregnant tern, Brooke Slocum, was being tortured by Oestrike in his basement where he had put her in handcuffs, wrapped in a chain around her neck and hooked her arms up to a pulley system suspended from the ceiling. He then sexually assaulted and tortured her, capturing the entire ordeal on film, before strangling her to death.

Then, when Oestrike realized the cops were closing in, he led police on a high speed car chase with Slocum's dead body stuffed in the trunk. After crashing his car into a railing, Oestrike fatally shot himself while sitting behind the wheel.

Oestrike's former live-in girlfriend told police that she met him via a Craigslist ad for a sex slave and escaped when Oestrike had chained her in the basement and shared his thoughts about killing her, telling her "These thoughts are happening to me." She escaped just in time.

138

Charles Clarke and Grant Muren

INCOMPATIBLE

In 2014, **Grant Van Muren,** 21, killed **Charles Clarke**, 55, met via Clarke's Craigslist ad seeking a roommate, and Muren moved into Clarke's townhouse. Just 8 hours later, in an argument following their sexual encounter, Muren hit Clarke on the head with a small table and then strangled him to death.

Clarke, a self-employed computer specialist, was described by neighbors as a "nice man" who had been living alone but had a girlfriend who occasionally visited him. Following the murder, Muren removed his personal belongings from the home, attempted to burn a lease agreement the two had drafted, by putting it in a toaster and turning it on, turned on the gas to the stove, and attempted to light 3 small fires in an attempt to cause an explosion. Clarke was discovered in the home with contusions to his face and head and the tips of one of his fingers appeared to have been bitten off.

The following day, Muren was pulled over for a traffic violation and was then charged with First Degree Murder and Concealing a Homicide. Muren claimed it was self defense. His 20-year sentence was reduced but he must serve half of a 14-year Murder sentence and spend 85% of the remaining 6-year sentence for Arson. He will be eligible for parole in 2024.

Kalynn Ruthenberg, Jordan Baker, Jonathan Myles   James Jones

ONE CON TOO MANY

On the evening of February 9, 2015, **James E. Jones**, 21, a chemistry student at Clark Atlanta University with aspirations to become a doctor, went to a residence on Jamaica Cove, Georgia, to purchase an iphone that had been advertised on Craigslist by **Kalynn Shiquez Ruthenberg**, 20, an associate of the Crips gang. Evidence showed that Ruthenberg and his two friends, **Jordan James Baker**, 18, and **Jonathan O'Neil Myles**, 19, had done this before as a way to rob the person responding to the ad. But this time, Ruthenberg shot and killed their robbery victim, Jones. As Jones lay dying, Ruthenberg told Baker and Myles to take Jones' Nike shoes off his feet and then shot him again.

Ruthenberg was convicted f Malice Murder and sentenced to Life Without Parole Plus 15 Years. Ruthenberg's co-defendants, Baker and Myles were each sentenced to 20 years.

Rene Leiva-Archila and Gregory Lewis

HALLOWEEN HOMICIDE

Gregory Lewis, 35, lured **Rene Leiva-Archila**, 44, and his son, 19, to a Baltimore parking lot by pretending to offer a car for sale for $1,700 in a Craigslist ad, on October 31, 2013.

When Archila arrived, Lewis ordered him to hand over his money and shot Archila to death with a shotgun. Archila's son fled on foot and called police.

Lewis pled guilty to First Degree Murder and Attempted Robbery and got "60 Years in Prison." He will then be 95 or will have already died in prison.

Natalie Bollinger and Joseph Lopez

BE CAREFUL WHAT YOU WISH FOR

Natalie Bollinger, 19, of Broomfield, Colorado, in a Craigslist post wrote: *"I want to put a hit on myself."* **Joseph Lopez**, 22, replied, using a hit man persona.

Bollinger told him Lopez would pay him to kill her "execution style." GPS data from Lopez' cell phone puts him in the remote woods where Bollinger died. Lopez told police he picked up Bollinger at her place and tried to talk her out of her plan. Eventually, they found the wooded area where they prayed before he shot her in the head with the gun she provided.

On December 28, 2017, 111 messages between Bollinger and Lopez were found on Bollinger's cell phone. Although an autopsy determined the single gunshot to the back of her head was cause of death, it also noted that Bollinger had "a potentially lethal dose of heroin in the blood at time of death." Lopez was being held without bail for Murder.

14

Grindr Graveyard

Stephen Port   Anthony Walgate, Daniel Whitworth, Jack Taylor, Gabriel Kovari

GRINDR'S SERIAL KILLER

Stephen Port, 41, a voracious sexual predator, would lure small, young, boyish looking men (known as "twinks"), via Grindr.com, to his London flat where he would drug them with GHB in their drinks and rape them after they were unconscious. The psychoactive drug was intentionally administered in fatal doses, leading to the deaths of four men: **Anthony Walgate**, 23, (his first victim, a fashion student and male escort); **Daniel Whitworth**, 21, who worked as a chef; **Jack Taylor**, 25, who lived with his parents and worked as a forklift driver; and **Gabriel Kovari**, 22, who briefly lived with Port. Port then left his victims' bodies near a churchyard about 500 feet from his home. He covered his tracks by discarding the men's phones, even planting their fake suicide notes, and also "blocked" one of his victims on Grindr and later deleted the Grindr app from his own phone.

Another victim, an unnamed 26-year old who survived, told jurors that Port twice injected him with a substance, without warning, using a plastic syringe. The victim objected, began to get dizzy, jumped off the bed and left. Port was known to surreptitiously use other drugs on his victims: Amyl Nitrite ("poppers"), Viagra, Mephedrone, Methamphetamine, and Crystal Meth.

Port's neighbor described him as having a peculiar, childlike personality, exhibiting odd behavior as a grown man, such as playing with children's toys. He came out as gay in the mid-2000s and worked as a chef.

On November 23, 2016, Port was convicted of Assaults By Penetration, Rapes and Murders of the four men and on November 25, 2016 he was sentenced to Life in Prison Without Parole.

Sean Crescentini and Fernando Rosales

LIFE OR SEX?

Sean Crescentini, 30, was contacted by **Fernando Rosales**, 34, on **Grindr** a month before they agreed to meet in person for a gay sex hook-up in the early hours of August 15, 2015 in Colorado Springs, Colorado. Rosales, a Fort Carson soldier who had served several tours of duty in Iraq and Afghanistan, earning the Army Commendation Medal, was called "selfless" and "among the best" by his superior officers.

Crescentini arrived at Rosales' home and began performing oral sex on Rosales while saying things to demean him, Rosales claimed. When Rosales started to get dressed, Crescentini allegedly lunged at him. Rosales admitted to fatally stabbing Crescentini once with a kitchen knife, alleging the older man had already punched him in the face after Rosales told Crescentini he was going to give his license plate number to police.

Crescentini managed to leave after suffering the moral wound, only to crash his Ford 250 pickup a few houses away. A police officer found him unresponsive behind the wheel and testified that the victim's intestines lay in his lap.

When a detective asked Rosales if he had thought about doing anything different, Rosales responded that he had thought about getting his gun.

Rosales was convicted of Second Degree Murder and sentenced to 26 Years in Prison.

Eric Michels   Gerald Matovu, Brandon Dunbar

CHEMSEX KILLERS

Eric Michels, 54, hooked up with **Gerald Matovu**, 26, via <u>Grindr</u> for sex at Michels' home, in August 2018. Matovu gave Michels a fatal dose of GHB (gama-hydroxybutric acid), also known as "the date rape drug" at his home in Chessington, then made off with Michels' bank card and other belongings.

Michels, an actor who had an uncredited role in the James Bond movie, "*Skyfall*," was the only one who died, of 12 men targeted by Matovu of Southwark, and his lover, **Brandon Dunbar**, 24, of Forest Gate, over a 19 month period. Ten of the victims had property stolen from them and 11 bank cards taken were used in fraudulent activities; eight of the victims were drugged with GBL, sold as an industrial cleaner which converts to GHB when in the body, to the point of unconsciousness. GHB, a prohibited drug, is often referred to as "liquid Ecstasy."

Matovu was found guilty of Michels' murder and a string of other offenses. Jurors were not told about Matovu's past connection with former chef and serial killer, **Stephen Port**, 44, from Barking, who had also targeted other victims through <u>Grindr</u> and killed them with GHB overdoses. In April 2017, Matovu had been sentenced to community service despite his past drug offences, after admitting he had sold and offered GHB to Port.

An Nuyen, Glenser Soliman

Brandon Lyons, Jerret Allen

TWO FOR ONE

An Vinh Nguyen, 26, a University of Houston student who was studying restaurant management, was last seen March 31, 2017. Nguyen's body has not yet been recovered and he is presumed dead. **Jerret Jamal Allen, 26,** was last spotted in April, 2013, using Nguyen's credit cards.

Prior to Nguyen's disappearance, the body of **Glenser Soliman**, 44, a male nurse who worked at St. Luke's Medical Center in Houston was found February 25, 2013, and **Brandon Alexander Lyons**, 18, Jerret Allen's cousin, was jailed and charged with stealing Soliman's car.

Authorities linked the two cousins and two victims, because both Lyons and Allen were in possession of property belonging to the two victims, Nguyen and Soliman, who, it is believed, were targeted because they were are Asian, were from Houston, and although the men's sexual orientation is unknown, it was believed that they had all connected via the gay dating app, Grindr, which had been linked to similar though non-lethal attacks in the Dallas area at the time.

backpage

(backpage.com)

murders = front page news

Damesha Hunt, Renisha Landers, Vernitha McCrary, Natasha Curtis - James C. Brown

2014 BACKPAGE MURDERS

James C. Brown, 25, of Sterling Heights, Michigan, was convicted of First Degree Murder in the killings of four Detroit women - **Damesha Hunt, Renisha Landers, Vernitha McCrary** and **Natasha Curtis** who he met through the adult classified advertising website, Backpage.com.

Brown was charged with 10 charges including First Degree Murder, Disinterment, Mutilation of a Dead Body and Arson in killings of the women in two separate incidents at his mother's Sterling Heights home and dumping the bodies in his old Detroit neighborhood. He caught rides home after dumping the women who were found in pairs – one pair having been set on fire. Wayne County Medical Examiners who ruled the deaths as Homicides testified they believed the women had been asphyxiated or suffered an asphyxiation type death and blood, DNA evidence and cell phone records helped prove Brown killed the women.

Brown told police that he smoked marijuana with the women, had sex with some of them, claimed he passed out and when he awoke, they were dead. But he admitted to putting their bodies in cars, driving them to Detroit and pouring gasoline on two of the bodies in the trunk and setting them on fire. He was sentence to mandatory Life in Prison.

Cynthia Worthy and Jerome Moore

2015 - BACKPAGE MURDER

Cynthia Worthy, 23, advertised on Backpage.com that she worked as a paid female escort under the name Lady." Cynthia was contacted for a date by **Jerome Moore**, 26, who lured her to his Oak Park, Michigan home on August 15, 2015. Worthy's sister reported her missing when Cynthia didn't return home from her date and because the sister works for OnStar, her family was able to track her car to Oak Park where it was found parked a block away from Moore's home. Cynthia Worthy's body was found two days later in a Detroit alley. She died of a single stab wound.

Prosecutors said cadaver dogs found Worthy's DNA in Moore's bedroom, on his shoes, in the basement and in the trunk of his car, which means she was still bleeding when she was in the car. Moor pleaded guilty to Second Degree Murder in exchange for dismissal of a First Degree Murder charge and was sentenced to 30 to 45 Years in Prison.

Following her death, Worthy's father told reporters his daughter wanted to give up escort work and had recently enrolled in college.

Desiree Robinson   Antonio Rosales,   Joseph Hazley,   Charles McFee

2016 BACKPAGE MURDER

The naked body of **Desiree Robinson**, 16, was found in a garage in Markham, Illinois, on Christmas Eve, 2016. She had been badly beaten and her throat cut. Two nights before, on December 23, **Antonio Rosales,** 32, from Chicago, found Desiree on Backpage.com and invited her to join him at a party that he and his sister were attending.

A witness told prosecutors that Rosales came to the party with friends and later had sex with Desiree in his truck. Rosales was arrested December 27 and told police he had no money for the second encounter and had tried to negotiate an additional free 15 minutes. She refused his offer and insulted him, so he punched her in the face, strangled her as she tried to call for help, then slit her throat.

At trial, **Charles McFee**, 26, admitted that he brought Desiree to a pimp, **Joseph Hazley**, for a $250 "finder's fee," days before she was murdered after being sold on Backpage.com. Hazley was said to be living in a car with his girlfriend when Desiree was murdered. McFee was offered a plea bargain to testify against Hazley for reduced sentence of only 6 to 8 years. McFee, who had no criminal history, cried in court over "somehow having got involved in something that got out of hand" and led to a 16 year old girl's death. McFee claims he never did get the $250 promised.

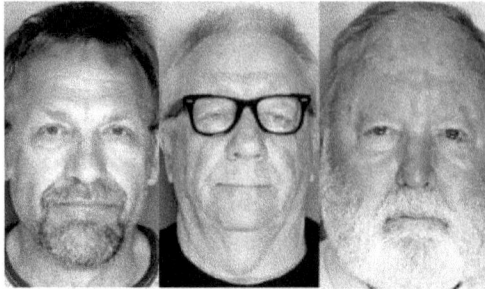
Carl Ferrer, Andrew Padilla, James Larkin

2018 - FEDS TAKE DOWN BACKPAGE

On April 6, 2018, federal authorities seized and took down Backpage.com after Texas Attorney General Ken Paxton's Law Enforcement Division arrested Backpage.com CEO, Carl Ferrer. They executed a search warrant on the Dallas headquarters of Backpage in 2015 and Ferrer, Andrew Padilla, Chief Operating Officer, and former Backstage owner, James Larken, were subpoenaed and testified at a 2017 Congressional hearing. All 3 pled guilty to Human Trafficking (of women and children) in Texas, and Money Laundering, through the sites they ran for 943 locations in 97 countries and 17 languages - which FBI agents began taking down all over the world.

Backpage had long been under fire from state attorneys general, organizations that fight child sex trafficking, and victims of the prostitution business who have tried to sue the company for damages. California prosecutors filed state criminal charges against Backpage in 2016 but that case was side-railed by protections of the federal 1996 Communications Decency Act (aka "Section 230"), for free speech on the internet. Anti-Sex Trafficking bills, House bill HR 1865, "Fight Online Sex Traffickers and Senate bill " (FOSTA), the "Stop Enabling Sex Traffickers Act" (SESTA) were signed into law by President Trump, April 11, 2018 (aka Public Law 115-164). ACLU fought the new measure as a "freedom of speech" issue, but Attorney Generals around the country had evidence of teenagers being trafficked. That's why, in 2018, Craigslist killed its "Personals" section.

With no way to find customers via internet, independent sex trafficking victims went back to pimps to work for less and 3 women were murdered as result of returning to street work. Other countries – Hong Kong, Argentina, Norway, Papua New Guinea – protect the human rights of people in the sex industry by the complete **decriminalization** of every aspect of **consensual** adult sex work and now there is virtually no sex trafficking in those countries – while in 2018-19, DHHS reports it "lost track" of 1475 children – 32 times the number sex trafficked in 2016.

backpage.com and affiliated websites have been seized

as part of an enforcement action by the Federal Bureau of Investigation, the U.S. Postal Inspection Service, and the Internal Revenue Service Criminal Investigation Division, with analytical assistance from the Joint Regional Intelligence Center.

Other agencies participating in and supporting the enforcement action include the U.S. Attorney's Office for the District of Arizona, the U.S. Department of Justice's Child Exploitation and Obscenity Section, the U.S. Attorney's Office for the Central District of California, the office of the California Attorney General, and the office of the Texas Attorney General.

Additional information will be provided at around 6:00 pm EST on Friday, April 6, by the U.S. Department of Justice, and all media inquiries should be directed to the U.S. Department of Justice's Office of Public Affairs at 202-514-2007 and press@usdoj.gov.

April 6, 2018

TAKEDOWN NOTICE

300 DATING & SEX ENCOUNTER EXPLOITATIVE APPS

Inclusion on this list is not intended as a recommendation. Some, not all are categorized. There are many more listings when Googled by subject.

Adam4Adam (gay)
Ads for Sex
Adult Date Link (sexual encounters)
AdultFriendFinder AFF.com (hookups)
AForeignAffair (Costa Rican)
Adult Hookup (sex)
Adult Match Firm (sex)
Adult Space (sex)
Adult XXX Date (sex)
Affair Dating (sex)
Aisle (Indian)
Align
ALT (bondage)
Amateur Community (sex)
Amateur Match (sex)
Amigos Ardientes (sex)
Amigis Clientes (sex)
AmoLatina
ArabLounge.com (Muslim)
AshleyMadison.com (sex encounters)
AsianDating.com
AYI (Are You Interested?)
BACKPAGE.com (shut down by FBI)
BADOO
BDSM (sado-masochism)
Beacon
Be Discreet (sex)
Bedpage.com (sex encounters)
BeNaughty (sex)
BiCupid (Bisexual)
BisexualFish.com
BlackCupid
Black People Meet (Black & biracial)
Black Planet
Black Sex Finder
Book of Sex

British Sex Contacts
Blendr
Blued (gay)
Bootyshake
Bold Personals (sex encounters)

Bristlr (Beards)
BUMBLE
Campus Flirts
Catholic Singles
C-date (sex)
Chappy (gay)
Chatville (adult)
Cheaters.net
Cheating Housewife
Cheeky Devil (sex)
Chemistry.com
ChristianCafe.com
ChristianConnection.com
ChristianCupid.com
ChristianDate.com
ChristianDatingForFree.com
ChristianMingle.com
ChristianPeopleMeet.com
Choppy (gay)
CityNews.com (Classified/Personals)
City Sex
ClassifiedAds.com (including sex)
Click and Flirt (sex)
Clover
Cmatch.com (Christian)
Coffee Meets Bagel
Compatible Partners
Conscious Singles
CRAIGSLIST (Community)
CrushZone (Teen)

157

Cupid (White)
Cute Hookup
DateHookup
Dating Affair
Dating.com
Dating For Muggies
Dating DNA
DesiKiss (Indian)
Dharma Match
Dig (for dog lovers)
Doublelist.com (sex encounters)

Down
Ebackpage (sex encounters)
EbonyFlirt (Black)
EDarling (German)
EHARMONY (Christian)
Elena's Models (Russian)
Elite Singles (College educated)
ELove Dates (Teen, free)
FACEBOOK
Facebook Dating
Feeld (group sex), 13,66,113
Fem
FindFlirt
FindMyFlings
FirstMet
Fling.com (sex)
Fliqpic
FlirtyMature (sex)
Flurv
FriendFinder-X
Free Hookups
Friendable
GayFriend Finder
Geebo (Classifieds/Personals)
Get It On (sex)
Get Naughty
Gk2Gk (Nerdy)
Gleeden (sex)
GRINDR (gay sex)
Grouper
Growlr (gay)
GuySpy (gay)
Happn
Hater
Helahel.com (Muslim)
Her (LGBQ)
158

HighThere (Get High & Maybe Sex)
Hily
Hinge
Hitch
Hoobly (Classified/Personals)
Hookup
Hookup Cloud
HookupEasyTonight
Hornet (gay)
Horny Matches
Horny Wife
HowAboutWe

Huggle
iCrushes (sex)
iHookup
Illicit Encounter
IndianCupid
Instant Hookups
Interracial Dating Central
Interracial People Meet
IwantU (sex)
Jack'd (gay)
Jaumo
Jcrush (Jewish)
JDATE (Jewish singles)
JDPeopleMeet (Jewish dating)
JewishCafe.com
JewishSoullSearch.com
Jmatch.com (Jewish
JPeopleMeet (Jewish)
JretroMatch.com (Jewish matchmaking)
IslamicMarriage.com (Muslim)
Jzoog.com (Jewish)
JustSayHi
JustHookup
Kijiji (like Backpage sex encounters)
Klique (sex)
LavaLife (Free)
Lumen (Seniors)
LatinLoveSearch
Latinolicious
Lay Mature
LesbianPersonals.com
Lesbotronic (Lesbian)
Lisa 18 (sex)
Locanto (Classifieds/Personals)
Lonely Cheating
LoveAholics (sex)

LoveAndSeek (Christian)
LoveHaibi.com (Muslim)
Luckyapp.co (sex encounters)
Lulu
LuvByrd (outdoorsy)
LuvSail (outdoorsy)
Mamba
Marital Affair (sex)
MATCH.com
MatureSinglesOnly (sex)
Meet4U
Meet24

Meet Locals (sex)
MEETME.com
Meet Native Americans
MenChats
Mingle2
Moonit
Muslima.com (Muslim)
Muzmatch (Muslim)
MyLOL (Teen)
MyLovelyParent
Native American Dating Service
Native American Passions
Native American Personals
Native Crush (Native American)
Naughty Adults
Naughty Date
99Flavors.com (swingers)
No Strings Attach
NoStrings.com.au (Australian)
No Strings Dating
Nudist Dating
OKCUPID (free)
Once
OnDaySix.com (Christian)
One Night Stand
OneScene (Lesbian)
Online Booty Call
Oodle.com (by physical appearance)
OurTime.com (Seniors)
OutdoorDuo (outdoorsy)
OutPersonals.com (gay date/hookup)
Parlor
Passion.com (sex)
Pennysaver (Classified/Personals)
Pernals (Personal ads)
Pheramor

Pickable
PinkSofa (Lesbian)
Planet Romeo (gay)
Play Naughty
PLENTY OF FISH (POF; Free)
Pure (Free)
QuackQuack (Indian)
Quick Flirt (sex)
Quiz Date Live (games)
RSVP.com.au (Australian)
Rude Finder (sex)
SalaamLove.com (Muslim)

Saucy Dates
SawYouAtSnai.com (Jewish)
Scout (sex)
Scruff (gay dating)
Shaddi.com (Indian)
Seeking Arrangement
SeniorFriendsDate
SeniorMatch
Sex Finder
Sex Play Cam
Sex Search
SilverSingles (Seniors)
SinceBeingSingle.com (Asian)
Single Parent Meet
Snapbang
Social Sex
SoulGeek (Nerdy)
SpeedDate
Spiritual Singles
Spoonr
StartSchmoozing.com (Jewish)
Stitch (Seniors)
SugarDaddyMeet
SugarDaddie.com
SuperTrova (Jewish)
Surge (gay)
Sweet Discreet (sex)
SweetRing
Swing Lifestyle
Swirlr (Interracial)
Tapdat (sex)
Tastebuds
Tease.com.au (Australian)
Teen Dating Site
TGPersonals (Transgender)
The Adult Hub (sex)

The Grade
The Inner Circle(Young professionals)
The League
3under (threesomes)
Tiami (gay)
TINDER
Tonight
TrulyAsian
Tryst.link (Independent escorts)TS
Dating (transgender)
TSMingle (transgender)
Tinder

Tingle (sex)
Tranny Dates
Trans Date
Trek Dating
TS TV Dates (Trans)
Twindog
Topface
Uberhorny
UK Classifieds
Ulust
Untrue (sex)
Up For It (sex)
Very Naughty
Want Ad Digest
WapLog
WhiteDate
Whovian Love
Well Hello (sex)
Whiplr
Wild
Wild Buddies (sex)
X Dating (sex)
X Match (sex)
Xpress
YesBackpage.com (like Backpage)
Zoe (lesbian)
Zoosk

BIBLIOGRAPHY

Anderson, Ryan, *"The Ugly Truth About Dating,"* Psychology Today, 9-6-16, and *"Are You Getting Enough Sex?"* Psychology Today, 4-25-`16

Balchunas, Caroline, *"Bonilla Guilty in 'MeetMe' Murder Trial Given Life Sentence,"* ABC News-4, 8-11-16

Beckman v. <u>Match.com</u>, Ninth Circuit Court of Appeals, No. 13-16324, filed 9-1-16.

Blunt, Rosie, *"Cyprus Serial Killer Case Exposes Abuse of Migrant Women,"* BBC News, 5-2-19

Bostock, Bill *"A British Man Killed His OKCupid Date in a Speedboat Accident, Went on the Run to Avoid Prison, and Turned Up 2,000 Miles Away on the Edge of Russia,"* Business Insider, 1-24-19

Brasch, Ben, *"Spiegel Guilty of Fort Meyers Beach Marina Double Murder,"* News-Press, 8-21-15

Brewer, John, *"Prosecutor Says Defendant Said 'I'm Famous. I'm the Craigslist Murderer,"* Twin Cities Pioneer Press, 3-23-09

Briquelet, Kate, *"Couple Murdered for Unfriending' Woman on Facebook,"* Daily Beast. 5-8-15

Buckley, Madeline, *"Richmond Hill Defendant Monserrate Shirley Gets 50 Years,"* Indy Star, 12-20-16

Bucktin, Christopher, *"Evil Killer Neil Entwistle Admits He Was in House When His Wife and Baby Were Shot Dead,"* Mirror, 1-23-16

CBS Staff, *"Police: Man Lured Shooting Victim With Craigslist Ad,"* CBS-4 WCCO-Minnesota 8-13-12; and *"Former Doctor Sentenced to More Than 36 Years in Drug Death of Pregnant Mother,"* CBS WBNS-10 TV, 12-20-13

Clearly, Tom, *"Watch: Elderly Man Shot and Killed in Cleveland in Facebook Video,"* Heavy.com, 4-18-17

Copeland, Dave, *"North Andover Victim Met Alleged Killer on Dating Site,"* Patch, North Andover, Massachusetts, 4-30-18

Cummings, Ian, *"Jury Recommends 32 Years in Prison for Teen Convicted in Killing During Gun Sale"* The Kansas City Star, 6-12-17

Curry-Reyes, Traciy, *"Jose Rodriguez-Cruz: 'Dateline NBC' The Golden Child Investigates Valentine's Day Killer,"* Dateline NBC, 3-1-19

De Simone, Daniel, *"The Link Between a Grinder Murderer And a Serial Killer,"* BBC News, 7-15-19

Domizio, Tony, *"Hatfield Man Accused of Killing Male Escort in Colorado,"* Montgomery-Lansdale Patch, 10-2-12

Duncan, Ian,, *"Man Convicted of Murdering Old Friend on Facebook,"* Baltimore Sun"1-3-13

Duthiers, Vladmir, *"Facebook Stalker Faces Trial for Model's Murder,"* CNN, 10-26-12

East, Rachel, *"Was Robyn Gardner, Missing Woman in Aruba, a Cheater or Prostitute?"* The Morton Report, 9-19-11

Edwards, Jim, *"The Facebook Killer: The Death of Jasmine Nunez and Social Media's Virtual Graveyard,"* Business Insider, 6-22-12

Ellicott, Clarie, *"The Schoolgirl Killed for a Bet: Boy, 16, Was Dared by Facebook Friend to

Murder in Exchange for Breakfast," Mail Online, 7-28-11

Faber, Tom, "*Grindr Has Transformed Gay Life, But Is It For The Better?*" The Face.com, June 27,2019

Feuerherd, Ben, "*George Zimmerman Gets Kicked Off Bumble, Again,*" New York Post, 2-11-19

Foo, Sasha, "*San Diego Woman Suffers Life Threatening Injuries After Tinder Date,*" KUSA-News San Diego, 4-11-18

Ghianna, Tim, "*Facebook 'Unfriending' Led To Double Murder, Police Say,*" Reuters, 2-9-12

Gibson, Suzy, "*Killers Who Lured Man to Industrial Estate by Promising Threesome Sentenced,*" LeicesterLive, 10-23-17

Gorrow, Chelsea, "*Eugene Man Allegedly Stabbed, Killed Woman He Met Online, Buried Body Under the Floorboards Before Going to Work*" The News-Review, 12-17-16

Grinberg, Emanuella, "*A Former UK Officer Was Convicted of Rape on a Tinder Date, But His Victims Says Trauma Is a 'Life Sentence,'*" CNN, 7-14-19

Grossman, Samantha, "*Woman Sues Match.com After Date Tries to Murder Her,*" TIME, 1-25-13

Hall, Christina, "*Michigan Man Convicted in Backpage.com Slayings,*" Detroit Free Press, 2-28-14

Hall, Louise, "*Facebook Killer Jailed for 21 Years,*" The Sydney Morning Herald 8-21-12

Hampton, Daniel, "*Parolee Met Woman on Plenty Of Fish; He's Accused of Killing Her,*" Flint Patch, 2-15-18

Harris, David, "*Woman's Killer Hid in Closet As She Slept Night Before Fatal Attack in Apopka Home,*" Orlando Sentinel, 7-20-18

Horseman, Jeff, "*Facebook Murder Case Defendant Concocted 'Sinister Plot' Prosecutor Says,*" The Press-Enterprise, 2-13-13

Hunt, Dave, "*Gable Tostee Found Not Guilty of Killing Warriena Wright on Tinder Date,*" ABC-au News, 10-20-16

John, Caroline, "*Ashley Pegram: South Carolina Woman Murdered By Her Kik Date, Edward Bonilla,*" Crimeola.com, 5-23-18

Kain, Eric, "*What Does the Facebook Double Homicide Say About the Dark Side of Social Media?*" Forbes, 3-11-12

Kazan, Olga, "*Nearly Half of All Murdered Women Are Killed by Romantic Partners (A New CDC Report Suggests that Domestic Violence is a Major Cause of Death for Women),*" The Atlantic (Health Archive), 7-20-17

Keach, Stacy, narrator, "*Inferno,*" (re Mark Leonard and Monserrate Shirley) American Greed, CNBC-TV, 8-14-17

Kemp, Joe, "*Two Brothers Charged With Killing Iraq War Vet Trying to Buy iPad; Pair Connected to Four Similar Attacks,*" New York Daily News, 12-10-13

Kragie, Andrew, "*Killers May have Used Dating App Like Grindr to Lure Victims, Detectives Say,*" San Francisco Chronicle, 8-8-17.

Lati, Marisa, "*Murder Suspect Slashes Own Throat in Court…,*" Washington Post, 6-25-18

Lien, A.T., "*2013 Straight From The A,*" Atlanta Entertainment Industry Gossip & News, 6-6-11

Linning, Stephanie, "*I Hope Her Story Can Save Others: Chilling Film About the*

Murder and Rape of Online Grooming Victim Kayliegh Hayworth Was Viewed More Than a Million Times," MailOnline, 1-4-17

Loiaconi, Stephen, *"Police: Suspects Wrote Texts, Facebook Messages,"* HLN -TV, 6-5-12

Lysiak, Matthew, *"Exclusive: Craigslist Killer Miranda Barbour Tells How and Why She Killed,"* Newsweek Magazine, 4-28-14

Magee, Ny, *"Maryland Man Arrested for Transferring HIV to Women He Met on Backstage and Bumble,"* The Grio.com. 4-16-19

Mann, Tanveer, *"Pictures Show Knife and Pick Axe Used to Kill Student by Tinder Date,* Metro News-U.K., 1-12-18

Margason, Greg, *"Georgia Man Charged With Murder in Death of Couple Seeking Car on Craigslist,"* FOX-59, 1-27-15

Martin, M.G., *"Cyprus Serial Killer – Whose Seven Victims Included Four Filippino Women – Gets Life,"* PLN News, 6-25-19

Martin, Patrick, *"'Craigslist Killer' Sentenced to 20 Years For Naperville Murder,"* Naperville (Illinois) Patch.com, 3-3-17.

McCai, Robert Stacy, *"MeetYourDeath.com: Psychopathic Killers Now Have Internet Access, you Know,"* TheOtherMcCain.com 12-3-12

McNab, Matt, *"1 Sentenced to Life, 1 Sentenced to 40 Years in Prison in Alex Apps Murder Case,"* The Beaumont Gazette, 8-26-18

Milam, Whitney, *"Wife Taken Out For Changing Facebook Status to Single,"* Metro News UK, Ranker, "The Absolute Craziest Deaths Caused by Social Media," 2008

Miller, Joshua Rhett, *"The Torture Chamber Where a Craigslist Threesome Ended in Death,"* New York Post, 11-7-16

Moore, Lane, *"Mass Murderer James Holmes's <u>Match.com</u> Profile Ws Terrifying,"* Cosmopolitan, 9-14-15

Moran, Lee, New York Daily News, *"Man, 20, Charged with Murder of Maine Teen Met Through Facebook,"* 5-22-13

Mourad, Sahar, *"'Fake' Doctor Accused of Raping His Bumble Date is Hit With More Dating App Sexual Assault Charges after Two More Women Come Forward with Similar Claims,"* Daily Mail, 12-11-18

Eal, Abra, *"Halifax Man Charged in Murder,"* Plympton-Halifax Express, 11-10-15

Newcomb, Alyssa, *"Facebook Murder Trial: Closing Arguments Set for This Week,"* The Nation 2-16-13"

Nix, Naomi, *"Markham Man Charged in Tinley Park Shooting,"* Chicago Tribune, 3-23-13

Parker, Andrew, *"Married Thug Raped Five Women He Met on <u>Match.com</u>, and had contacted Thousands More,"* The Sun, 3-3-16

Paul, Deanna, *"Bumble and Tinder Refuse to Help Trayvon Martin's Killer Look For Love,"* The Washington Post, 4-19-19

Paul, Jesse, *"Former Soldier Gets 26 Years in Prison for Fatal Colorado Springs Stabbing,"* Denver Post, 12-6-16

Pidd, Helen, *"Online Daters Warned to Avoid Murder Suspect – Women Told Not to Meet Up with George Appleton After Young Mother's Burnt Body Found in Manchester Flat,"* The Guardian, 2-10-09

Pointer, Jack, *"Man's Dating Site Hookup Ended in Murder, Court Documents Show,"* 4-18-18

Powell, Jaya, "*How Not to Get Killed By Your Tinder Date*," bolde.com/jayap

Ray, Esha, Nancy Dillon, Reuven Blau and Janon Fisher, "'*He Was a Cool Guy' Says L.I. Woman Who Cheated Death at Hands of Suspected Serial Killer Who Admits to Killing Seven*," New York Daily News, 7-30-18

Rafferty, Jillian, "John Charlton Charged with 1st Degree Murder of Renton Mom."

Reditz, Heidi, "*Is Your Date Deadly? Here's How to Find Out*," Infomania.com, 1-16-19

Reynolds, Trench, "*December Criagslist Murder in Indy Over An iPhone*," The Trench Reynolds Report, 1-25-13; and "*Brothers Please Guilty to Grisly Double Craigslist Murder*," The Trench Reynolds Report, 5-11-19

Riggins, Alex, "*Attorney: Accused Accomplice in Craigslist Murder Was Unaware of Killer's Ambush Plot*," MV MagicValley.com, 7-25-16

Roberts, Michael, "*Draton Mares, ex-Craigslist Hookup, Guilty of Globetrotters Trainer Thomas Bashline's Death,*" Westword.com. 10-26-12

Romano, Aja, "*Man Who Murdered Online Date Had 900 Facebook Friends*," The Daily Dot, 2-25-17; and "*A New Law Intended to Curb Sex Trafficking Threatens the Future of the Internet As We Know It*," VOX.com, 7-2-18

Rosenberg, Rebecca, "*Inside Alleged Wife-Killer's Twisted Plans to Get Away With Murder*," New York Post, 1-21-19

Rubin, Paul, "*Wade Ridley, Match.com 'Hunter' Who Killed Phoenix Woman Apparently Commits Suicide in Nevada Joint*," Phoenix New Times, 5-7-12

Rustling, Jimmy, "*Woman Kills Five People for Not Accepting Friend Requests on Facebook*," Super Official News, 2-25-13

Santschl, Darrell, "*San Jacinto: Jury Convicts Facebook Killer*," The Press-Enterprise, 2-20-13

Schladebeck, Jessica, "*Man Accused of Killing and Dissolving Tinder Date's Body in Acid Arrested in Mexico City*," New York Daily News, 12-26-16

Schupp, Kimberly, "*Another Craigslist Killer? Bodied of 4 Women ID'd*," CBS-WTOL-11 TV, 2011

Sennett, Desiree, "*Thomas 'Mike' Heath Found Guilty of Murder in Case of Slain Disney Worker*," Orlando Sentinel, 8-2-13

Shaddi, Abusaid, "*2 More Sentenced in Craigslist Killing*," Marietta Daily Journal, 3-2-18

Sharp, David, "*Teens Wary of Facebook Following Classmate's Murder*," NBC News, 5-31-13

Shay, Miya, "*Charges Dropped Against Teen Accused of Luring Shooting Victim*," Eyewitness News, ABC-TV-13, 7-10-15

Sigona, Michelle, "*Match Made in Hell: 5 Internet Dates That Ended in Murder*," ID TV Crime Feed, 3-3-16

Smith, Catherine, "*Serial Sex Offender Admits Using Facebook to Rape and Murder Teens*," Huffington Post, 5-8-10

Sokmenseur, Harriet, "*Illinois Man Allegedly Advertised Sex With Pregnant Wife, Then Fatally Shot the Man Who Showed Up*," People.com. 8-1-1

Staples, Gracie Bonds, "*2 Riverdale Teens Held in Death of Lithonia Man Selling iPhone*," The Atlanta Journal-Constitution, 11-9-13

Stickney, R., "*Donna Jou Killing: John Burgess Released From Prison*," NBC-7 News-San Diego, 7-30-15

Stokes, Paul,"*Ashleigh Hall: One Mistake Cost Teenager Her Life*," The

Telegraph (UK),3-8-10

Stout, Steve, "*Man Gets 27 Years in Prison for Murder, Burglary of Scottsdale Woman,*" AZ Family, 5-8-15

Telegraph, The, Staff Writer, "*Man Murdered Wife 'After She Changed Her Facebook Status to Single,'*" Wales News Service, The Telegraph, 9-1-09

Thompson, Paul, "*Triple Murderer Caught After One of His Alleged Victims Posted on Her Facebook Page Moments Before He Shot Her,*" Mail Online, 1-24-12

Thurson, Jack, "*Vt. Woman Sentenced For Car Crash Killing – Online Dating Chats Helped Crack the Case,*" NBC-5, 11-2-12

Tobin, Olivia and Sean Morrison, "*Laureline Garcia-Bertaux Death: Man Denies Murder of Woman Found Buried in Shallow Grave in Kew,*" Evening Standard, (U.K.), 6-11-19

Urycki, Mark, "*Akron's Craigslist Killer is Sentenced to Death,*" WKSU-Radio 89.7, 7-14-19

Vercammen, Paul, "*California Man Who Allegedly Stuck Dates With the Check Faces Years in Prison,*" CNN, 9-3-18

Walsh, Michael, "*Wannabe Hero's Plot Ends in Tragedy; Kyle Dube Charged with Nichole Cable's Death,*" New York Daily News, 5-30-13

Warran, Beth, "*Craigslist Shooting Victim Described as Devoted Dad, 'The Good One,'*" The Commercial Appeal, and Material Reader, 4-28-14

Warren, Sabian, "*Woman Sentenced in Asheville Slaying Tied to Craigslist Ad,*" Citizen-Times, 12-3-14

Weill, Kelly, "*Accused Killer: Teen Posted a Craigslist Ad Asking to Be Murdered,*" DailyBeast.com, 2-11-18

West, Alex, "*Plenty Of Fish Killer Stabbed Woman to Death – Then Hunted for More Victims,*" The Sun, 3-21-18

Wigglesworth, Valerie, "*Expert in Capital Murder Trial Testifies Terrance Black's DNA Found in Ex-Girlfriend's Car,*" Frisco Rough Rider, August 2012 issue.; and "*Terrance Black Guilty of Murder of Frisco Fitness Instructor,*" Dallas News, 8-8-12.

Wikipedia, "*Mark Twitchell.*"

Wootson Jr., Cleve R., "*Police: Man Killed After Meeting Woman on PlentyOfFish Dating Site,*" SFGate.com. 8-25-16.

Wright, Matthew, "*Man Admits He Brought 16 Year Old to Pimp For $250 'Finders Fee' Days Before She Was Murdered After Being Sold on Backpage.com,*" Mail Online, 4-3-18

Wu, Sydney, "*Millersville Man Sentenced for Craigslist Murder, Apologizes to Family,*" Maryland Patch.com, 2-18-15

Young, Stephen, "*Bryant Guilty in 2016 Murder of TWU Student Jaqueline Vandergriff,*" Dallas Observer, and Dallas Morning News, 4-16-16

Zaczek, Zoe and Alex Chapman, "*Divorced father-of-Two, 37, Who Masqueraded as a Doctor, is Accused of Raping a Woman, 26, After Meeting on Bumble Date,*" Daily Mail Australia, 8-30-18

INDEX

ABOUT THE AUTHOR

LORI CARANGELO retired from administrative postions in Santa Barbara and Palm Desert, California, and authored 25 non-fiction adoption-themed and true crime books.

Lori is also no stranger to murder and murderers. As biographer to several serial killers, her "ripped from the headlines" murder stories provide a voice to both the victims and their killers, to explain not only how but also why it happened, and also how to prevent creating or enabling more "monsters."

More Books by Lori Carangelo:

SCHOOL SHOOTERS
Why They Did It and America's War on Guns

ADOPTED KILLERS
430 Adoptees Who Killed - How and Why They Did It

SERIAL KILLERS ON THE INTERSTATE
200 Highway Killers by State

KONDRO
The "Uncle Joe" Killer

EYEWITNESS
The Case of the Carefully Crafted Central Coast Rapist

BLOOD RELATIVES
A True Story of Family Secrets and Murders

JAMES MUNRO
And the Freeway Killers

RAGE!
How an Adoption Ignited a Fire

CHOSEN CHILDREN
*Children as Commodities in America's
Failed Foster Care, Adoption and Immigration Systems*

ESPOSITO
The First Mafioso

THE ULTMATE SEARCH BOOK
*U.S. and World Editions
Adoption, Genealogy and Other Search Secrets*

THE ADOPTION and DONOR CONCEPTION FACTBOOK
*The Only Comprehensive Source of U.S. & Global Data
On the Invisible Families of Adoption, Foster Care
& Donor Conception*

THE 8 BALL CAFÉ
Stories of Adoption, Addiction and Redemption

www.ingramcontent.com/pod-product-compliance
Lightning Source LLC
Chambersburg PA
CBHW071533040426
42452CB00008B/1005